Make your
PAYCHECK
Last

How to
Create
a Budget
You Can
Live With

Jason R. Rich

CAREER
PRESS
Franklin Lakes, NJ

MAKE YOUR PAYCHECK LAST
EDITED BY CLAYTON W. LEADBETTER
TYPESET BY EILEEN DOW MUNSON
Cover design by Dorothy Wachtenheim
Printed in the U.S.A. by Book-mart Press

To order this title, please call toll-free 1-800-CAREER-1 (NJ and Canada: 201-848-0310) to order using VISA or MasterCard, or for further information on books from Career Press.

The Career Press, Inc., 3 Tice Road, PO Box 687,
Franklin Lakes, NJ 07417
www.careerpress.com

Library of Congress Cataloging-in-Publication Data

Rich, Jason.
    Make your paycheck last : how to create a budget you can live with / by
Jason R. Rich.
        p. cm.
    Includes index.
    ISBN 1-56414-699-5 (pbk.)
    1. Finance, Personal. 2. Budgets, Personal. I. Title.

HG179.R445 2004
332.024—dc21

                                                                2003054649

Acknowledgments

One of the keys to success in life is to surround yourself with smart, creative, and caring people you love and who provide endless support. Mark, the Bendremer family (Ellen, Sandy, and Emily), along with Ferras, are the closest and dearest friends anyone could ever hope for. For their friendship I am truly grateful. Their collective friendship means so much more than having lots of money...although being disgustingly rich would be nice too! I'd also like to express my love and gratitude to my family, who have remained extremely supportive of me throughout the years, even when times got tough.

Thanks also to Ron Fry, Mike Lewis, Clayton Leadbetter, Eileen Munson, Kirsten Beucler, Stacey Farkas, Gina Cheselka, and everyone else at The Career Press, for helping to bring *Make Your Paycheck Last* into print and for inviting me to work on this project.

Contents

Introduction

re you like so many other people who earn a steady income, yet continue to struggle in order to pay your everyday living expenses and meet all of your financial obligations? Perhaps you've recently been laid off or were suddenly forced to make due with less financially. Whatever your personal (or family) financial situation, *Make Your Paycheck Last* is all about better utilizing the money you have, in order to meet your obligations and improve your overall financial situation. As you'll see, it's also about preparing for the future and developing plans for achieving your true earning potential.

Learning how to better manage your finances isn't difficult. In fact, there are countless strategies you can implement quickly and easily that are virtually guaranteed to improve your financial situation. For most people, the difference between being financially stable and having serious financial troubles comes down to having a basic knowledge of how to develop and implement a budget into their daily lives, plus having the motivation and willingness to faithfully adhere to that budget. Learning how to be responsible with your money, by controlling spending, increasing savings, and reducing (or eliminating) your debt, is information you will learn from this book.

Obtaining the information you need, however, is just step one. The next step is to take an active approach when managing your finances and immediately start applying what you learn. There is no place for laziness or carelessness when it comes to successfully managing your finances and making your paycheck last!

Once you start applying this information on an ongoing basis, you *will* see positive results. The trick is to take a well-organized and thought-out approach to improving and managing your financial situation, even if you're not a mathematical genius and the amount of your paycheck isn't what it could or should be.

You, Too, Can Benefit From This Book

Make Your Paycheck Last was written for anyone and everyone who needs or wants to improve their financial situation. The strategies you're about to read apply to:

▶ Anyone trying to make ends meet in the midst of a poor economy.

▶ Business professionals who want to get the most out of the money they're earning.

▶ Homemakers who need to stretch every dollar in order to maintain a comfortable standard of living for themselves and their families.

▶ Newlyweds first establishing their family's finances.

▶ People attempting to reduce or eliminate a large amount of debt.

▶ Recent graduates first entering the working world.

▶ Recently divorced people who need to rework their entire financial plan, without their former spouse in the picture.

▶ Recently laid-off (or downsized) workers who are forced to deal with a sudden loss or reduction of income.

▶ Single parents forced to juggle a personal and professional life.

▶ Students forced to live on a budget and establish their financial independence.

Personal Finances Versus Family Finances

There's little difference between developing and implementing a personal budget (for yourself) and a budget for your family. To successfully develop a family budget and manage your family's finances, it's critical that you and your spouse are always on the same page, in terms of understanding your family's financial situation and what needs to be done to improve it. When making cuts in your spending habits, for example, the reductions or eliminations you make should be agreed upon by you and your spouse. If there's total agreement, in terms of the sacrifices that need to be made and the spending habits that need to be altered in order to achieve your goals, your chances of success will be much greater.

After all, there's little point in creating a budget by yourself, saving money throughout the month, then having your spouse go on an unnecessary spending spree at the mall because he or she didn't understand or agree with the financial decisions you've made.

If your children are old enough to understand the financial situation your family faces, you might consider involving them in certain financial decisions, especially as you work toward establishing and maintaining a family budget and look for ways to successfully reduce spending without negatively impacting your standard of living too much.

What You'll Need When Reading This Book

As you read this book, keep a pen and pad of paper nearby. It's also a good idea to gather together all of your personal (or family) financial records—checkbook, bills, bank statements, paycheck stubs, tax returns, and so on, so you'll be able to calculate accurate answers as you complete the various worksheets throughout the book. A calculator or personal computer (with personal finance software such as Microsoft Money or Quicken) will also be useful to have at your disposal.

What to Expect From This Book

Each chapter of this book focuses on a different aspect of your finances. Chapter 1 is all about evaluating your current financial situation and gathering together a list of your expenses. It's also about setting realistic and achievable financial goals. Once you know what your financial situation is like right now, Chapter 2 focuses on developing a personal or family budget, setting priorities in terms of your spending habits, finding ways to cut expenses, learning how to balance your checkbook, and also discusses the importance of creating a plan for savings. You'll also learn about popular personal finance software packages you can use with your computer to make your money management easier.

Chapter 3 deals with issues relating to debt and focuses on effectively using (not abusing) credit cards, establishing and maintaining your credit, and developing strategies for reducing and, ultimately, eliminating the debt you've already acquired. Chapter 4 focuses on how to deal with unexpected financial hardship and financial emergencies. It also describes things you can do to protect yourself financially when something negative happens.

In Chapter 5, you'll discover that becoming thrifty in terms of your spending habits doesn't mean you magically transform into a cheapskate. This chapter offers advice and strategies for saving money in your every-day life, plus it offers tips for planning for your financial future. Finally, Chapter 6 focuses totally on the future. It describes things you can start doing right now in order to eventually improve your earning potential, make more money, and ultimately, achieve your long-term financial goals.

Ideally, as you read this book, you'll want to immediately begin taking better control of your current financial situation and work toward getting yourself out of any financial troubles you're currently facing (such as excessive credit card debt). At the same time, start planning for the future and take steps to improve your financial well-being and earning potential in the months and years to come.

Everyone's personal or family situation is different. This book will help you develop strategies that will help to improve your finances, but you'll often need to adapt various strategies so they better apply to your own situation. For example, when it comes to finding ways to cut your everyday expenses, feel free to use your own creativity to discover ways you can save money, without negatively impacting your current standard of living. What's offered here is a collection of ideas and strategies you can use as a starting point.

As you discover what works for you, please feel free to share your discoveries by e-mailing me at jr7777@aol.com. Perhaps your budgeting or money-saving strategies could help other people and would be suitable for a future edition of this book.

To get the most out of this book, read it in its entirety first, then go back and read it one chapter at a time as you complete the various worksheets and start developing your own budget. Remember, as you begin to incorporate the various financial strategies that are designed to help make your paycheck last, do only one or two things at a time. Don't overwhelm yourself by taking on too much at once. Focus on fixing the worst aspects of your personal financial situation first, and don't be afraid to seek out the help and guidance of a financial specialist (see Appendix A for details). Whether you're earning minimum wage or millions of dollars per year, you have the power to take control over your finances and manage them successfully!

—Jason R. Rich
www.JasonRich.com

Who Wants
to Be a Millionaire?
I Do!

Have you practically dedicated your life to working for a paycheck that barely covers your cost of living? Do you feel like the majority of your life is spent on the job? Does virtually every penny you earn get spent on necessities, with little or nothing left over after each pay period? Have you been relying on credit cards to help make ends meet? Do you find yourself getting deeper and deeper into debt, with no relief in sight? Have you been negatively impacted by the slow economy, forced to pay higher prices for what you need, while, at the same time, you're earning less money?

This, unfortunately, is the financial situation faced by countless millions of people, from all walks of life. While there are no magical answers for quickly getting yourself out of debt or guaranteed ways of building wealth, once you fully understand the financial situation you're in, there are strategies you can easily implement that will help you more easily meet your financial obligations and achieve your realistic financial goals.

When it comes to making your paycheck last and building wealth, you must understand these basic realities: First, there are no easy solutions. Second, improving your current financial situation is going to take hard work, proper planning, plus a major commitment and effort on your part.

So, unless you happen to win the lottery or receive a large inheritance from a long lost relative, if you want to receive the maximum benefits from the money you have, you'll need to plan and strategize properly.

This book is all about taking the money you have and making it work harder for you. It's also about planning for the future and constantly working to improve your overall financial situation, one step at a time. This chapter, for example, focuses on helping you to better understand your current financial situation, based on the quality of life you're living right now. It will also help you explore what you want from the future, so you can set attainable short-term and long-term financial goals, plus develop and implement well-thought-out strategies for achieving those goals.

The good news is, you don't need to become an accountant or financial wizard to discover how to better manage your money, control your spending, develop a saving/investment plan, and make your paycheck last. Anyone can follow the basic strategies outlined in this book and discover just some of the secrets for living a more financially stable life.

Your Current Quality of Life

"Quality of life" can mean many things. For example, it can refer to your level of happiness, the stability of your marriage and family life, the value of your possessions, how comfortable you are in terms of your standard of living, how educated you are, and/or how much money you earn. If you drive through Beverly Hills, California and see someone living in a multimillion dollar home, driving a top-of-the-line Mercedes, and wearing the latest designer fashions, you might believe that they've achieved an excellent quality of life. After all, the person living in Beverly Hills has managed to purchase some of the best things money can buy.

We all have dreams of living a lifestyle like the rich and famous. For most people, however, our day-to-day reality keeps us living a vastly different lifestyle, and we need to pay constant attention to every penny that's being spent in order to make ends meet. Before you can begin implementing strategies to help you better manage your money, cut spending, boost savings, and improve your overall financial stability, you need to develop a thorough understanding of what your financial situation is like right now.

So, are you ready to get started? As you complete the financial worksheets in this chapter and elsewhere in this book, you'll need a calculator, pen, and paper, plus copies of your monthly bills and financial statements. Don't worry, in terms of financial calculations, you won't be asked to do anything more than basic addition and subtraction. If you own a computer, however, using a program such as Microsoft Money or Intuit Quicken (described in Chapter 2) can make developing and maintaining your personal or family finances much easier.

Your Current Financial Situation

Developing a true understanding of your current financial situation is the first step to making your paycheck last and building greater wealth in the future. Evaluate your current financial situation means developing a thorough understanding about:

▶ How much money you have now—in savings and investments, for example.

▶ How much money you're presently earning (your income).

▶ What your current debts, expenses, and liabilities are.

First, let's create an accurate "net worth statement." This is a detailed listing of what you own (your assets) and your debts (liabilities). Complete the worksheet on page 16 to the best of your ability. This first worksheet will help you determine your current net worth. Once the worksheet is complete, to determine your net worth, subtract the total value of your liabilities from the total value of your assets.

TOTAL ASSETS – TOTAL LIABILITIES = NET WORTH

If the total value of your assets is greater than your liabilities, you have a positive net worth (you're worth more than you owe). If the value of your assets is lower than your liabilities, you have a negative net worth. It's very common for people with a mortgage and various types of loans, for example, to have a negative net worth.

Net Worth Statement Worksheet

Asset Description	Value ($)
Cash in Savings Account(s)	
Cash in Checking Account(s)	
Current Cash Value of Life Insurance	
Current Equity in Your Home, Condo, or Apartment(If applicable)	
Value of Car(s)	
Value of Investment(s)(Mutual Funds, Stocks, Bonds, CDs, Commodities, etc.)	
Value of Personal Property	
Value of Retirement Account (IRA, Keogh, etc.)	
Other Assets	
TOTAL:	

Liability Description	Value ($)
Bank Loan(s)	
Car Loan(s)	
Credit Card Balance(s)	
Mortgage Balance	
Personal Loan(s)	
Other Liabilities	
– TOTAL:	

YOUR CURRENT NET WORTH: $ _____

One of your long-term financial goals (to be discussed later in this chapter) should be to ultimately achieve a positive net worth. As you begin taking steps to adjust your spending, save money, reduce your debt, and improve your overall financial situation, you'll want to recalculate your net worth every few months. This will help you track your progress.

Knowing your net worth is important. It allows you to look at the big picture in terms of your financial situation. For the short term, it's more important to understand how much money you're earning each month and determining exactly how you're spending the money you receive from each paycheck. To help you calculate this information, complete the worksheets on pages 17–20.

Monthly Income Worksheet

Directions: Complete this worksheet using income from a one-month period. You can also take your annual net income (take-home pay) and divide it by 12 to determine your average monthly income.

Income Type	Value ($)
Take-Home Pay & Earned Income (Salary After Taxes)	
Spouse's Take-Home Pay & Earned Income(Salary After Taxes)	
Child Support/Alimony Received	
Interest, Capital Gains, and Dividend Earnings From Investments	
Pension/Retirement Income	
Social Security (Income Received)	
Other Income	
TOTAL:	

Monthly Expense Worksheet

Directions: A *fixed expense* is one that is the same every month, such as your rent or mortgage. *Flexible expenses* can vary from month to month. Using the worksheets provided, calculate all of your fixed expenses (shown on the first chart), followed by your flexible expenses (on the following page). Ideally, you'll want to track your spending carefully for three to six months, by completing these worksheets each month, to ultimately determine how your money is being spent.

Fixed Expenses Month:_____ Year: _____	
Type of Expense	Cost ($)
Auto Insurance	
Car Payment	
Disability Insurance	
Home Insurance (Renter's Insurance)	
Life Insurance	
Medical/Health Insurance	
Other Loan Payment(s)	
Rent/Mortgage	
Alimony/Child Support Payments	
Payment to Savings for Child's College	
Payment to Retirement Account(s)	
Investment to Stocks, Mutual Funds, etc.	
#1 TOTAL:	

Flexible Expenses Month:_____ Year: _____	
Type of Expense	Cost ($)
Cable TV Bill	
Cellular Phone Bill	
Childcare/Babysitting	
Clothing	
Commuting Costs	
Credit Card Payments	
Dining out/Take-out Food Expenses	
Donations to Charities	
Dues for Clubs, Organizations, and Religious Institutions	
Education	
Electric Bill	
Entertainment/Recreation Expenses	
Food and Groceries	
Fuel Bill	
Gas Bill	
Gas for Vehicle(s)	
Gifts	
Home Maintenance/Upkeep Costs	
#2 TOTAL:	

Flexible Expenses Month:_____ Year:_____	
Type of Expense	Cost ($)
Internet Connection Fees	
Laundry/Dry Cleaning	
Medical, Prescriptions, and Dental Expenses	
Newspapers, Magazines, and Books	
Parking for Your Vehicle(s)	
Personal Care and Grooming Products/Fees	
Pet Supplies and Expenses (Vet, Food, Grooming, etc.)	
Taxes (Real Estate, etc.)	
Telephone Bill	
Trash Removal	
Vacations	
Vehicle Maintenance	
Water Bill	
Other Expenses	
#3 TOTAL:	
#1 TOTAL:	$_____
#2 TOTAL:	$_____
#3 TOTAL:	$_____
GRAND TOTAL:	$

By adding up all of your fixed and flexible expenses, you can determine how much money you need to earn per month to maintain your current lifestyle and quality of life. Now take this figure (total expenses) and subtract it from your total monthly income. Do this basic calculation to determine your net available cash flow (also called your *discretionary income*):

Total Income – All Expenses (Fixed and Flexible) = Net Available Cash Flow

---

If each month you're earning more than you need to survive and maintain your current quality of life, you're starting off in good shape. This means you have discretionary income at your disposal because your net available cash flow is a positive number. Next, determine the best ways to improve your quality of life and properly invest or utilize this leftover money each month, while, at the same time, you discover ways to cut your spending to save additional money.

For a multitude of reasons, many people find themselves spending more each month than they earn. Thus, to cover expenses, they're forced to tap their savings and/or use credit cards to make up the difference. In this situation, there is no discretionary income. This means you're living beyond your means and need to take steps to avoid financial disaster before it's too late. These steps might be as simple as cutting a few costs. Based on the severity of the situation, it might require a drastic change to your spending habits and lifestyle in order to get your financial situation under control. Chapters 2, 3, 4, and 5 provide strategies for learning to better manage your finances.

Defining Your Goals

Do you have dreams of living in a nicer place, driving a luxury car, wearing designer clothes, traveling to exotic places, and dining in the finest restaurants, only to have those dreams squashed each time you pay your monthly bills and have little or nothing left over? The first step to achieving your financial dreams is to set short-term and long-term goals for yourself that are realistic and achievable. Next, develop and implement a well-thought-out plan for achieving each of your goals, taking one step at a time.

If, for example, one of your long-term goals is to be debt free, one of the first steps to take is to begin paying off your high interest loans, such as your outstanding credit card balances. Just think, if that same money was being invested instead of paying high interest rates each month, your net worth would grow quickly.

Throughout this book are proven tricks for achieving financial success. However, before you proceed, it's important to define what "success" means to you. Does achieving success mean becoming a highly paid executive or being able to retire at a young age as a multimillionaire? Does it mean having a career you truly love? Does achieving success mean getting married, having kids, and then earning a living to support your family? Does it mean buying an expensive house and a sports car?

Everyone has a different definition for what constitutes success. Here's how the *Merriam-Webster's Collegiate Dictionary* defines this term: "Degree or measure of succeeding; favorable or desired outcome; the attainment of wealth, favor or eminence; one that succeeds."

Take a few minutes and define *success* for yourself:

What's your definition of *personal* success?

_____

_____

_____

_____

_____

_____

_____

What's your definition of *professional* (career-related) success?

_____

_____

_____

_____

_____

_____

_____

What's your definition of *financial* success?

_____

_____

_____

_____

_____

_____

_____

_____

What's your *overall* definition of success?

_____

_____

_____

_____

_____

_____

_____

_____

Just as athletes have coaches who offer them guidance, training, and motivation, when you set out to better manage your personal finances, it's often a good idea to seek out the advice of a financial expert, such as an accountant, CPA (Certified Public Accountant), Certified Financial Planner, stock broker, or investment specialist who can act as your financial coach and help you make educated decisions about your spending and investing. However, just as in sports, a coach can't force an athlete to excel. If you want to achieve financial success, you'll need to take action and responsibility for yourself.

While it's perfectly acceptable to seek out guidance, support, and help from others, one of the biggest mistakes people make is becoming too reliant on other people. While you may occasionally want support or help from others when it comes to achieving your goals, consider this help a bonus. Ultimately, it must be you who will determine to what degree you're able to achieve your financial objectives.

No matter who you are, how successful you've already become, how well-educated you are, or what type of personality you have, developing specific goals and constantly working toward achieving those goals are among the key ingredients for achieving financial success. As you define what your personal, professional, and financial goals are, make sure those goals are your own, and that they're realistic.

Based upon where you are in your life right now, write down specific goals you have for yourself in the following three areas:

▶ Personal Goals—Relating to your family, friends, health, overall well-being, education, and life outside of work.

▶ Professional Goals—Relating to your career or job.

▶ Financial Goals—Relating to anything and everything that has to do with money.

You'll probably discover that your financial goals are directly related to your personal and/or professional goals. For example, if one of your personal goals is to buy a home (apartment or condo) in five years, you'll need to adjust your financial goals accordingly to accommodate that expense. Likewise, if your financial goals involve ultimately earning more money than you do right now, you'll need to adjust your career-related goals to ensure upward mobility in the career you've selected for yourself.

As you define your goals, consider a short-term goal as something you want to achieve within the next 12 months. A long-term goal is something that will take more than one year to achieve. Now, as you contemplate your goals, make sure they're realistic. After all, if you're earning $30,000 per year and your annual expenses are $28,000 per year, having the goal of acquiring $1,000,000 in savings over the next five years probably isn't too practical or achievable. Think carefully about what your goals are and what steps you'll need to take in order to achieve them.

Goal-Setting Tips

▶ Start off by considering your long-term goals and write them down.

▶ Take each long-term goal and divide it into a series of more easily achievable short-term goals.

▶ Create a game plan, starting immediately, for reaching each short-term goal. What can you begin doing, starting right now, to achieve that goal? It might help to create a checklist or divide each goal into 10 steps, for example.

▶ Prioritize your goals and the steps needed to achieve them. Focus the majority of your energy on achieving the goals that are the most important.

▶ Set a time frame for achieving each goal. Create specific deadlines and work toward meeting those dates.

▶ Keep your goals somewhat flexible, because life is full of uncertainties. As changes in your life take place (for better or worse), be able to adjust your goals accordingly.

▶ Keep a written journal or diary of your progress as you work toward and achieve each goal.

▶ Refer to your list of goals regularly to keep you on track, focused, and motivated.

Personal Goals

As the title suggests, personal goals deal primarily with education, self-improvement, relationships, and family issues. To help you define your goals, you might start your sentence with a phrase such as "I wish..." or "I plan to..."

Short-Term Personal Goals:

_____

_____

_____

_____

_____

Long-Term Personal Goals:

_____

_____

_____

_____

_____

Professional Goals

Professional goals deal with job or career-related issues. They might concern promotions, transfers, pay raises, your overall career path, or even occupational changes.

Short-Term Professional Goals:

_____

_____

_____

_____

_____

_____

Long-Term Professional Goals:

_____

_____

_____

_____

_____

_____

Financial Goals

Your financial goals have to do with money, investments, and assets. These goals should relate directly to your income, expenses, and how you invest your money. For example, paying off your credit card debt over the next three years or developing a plan to pay for your 12-year-old child's college education would be considered long-term financial goals.

Short-Term Financial Goals:

_____

_____

_____

_____

_____

Long-Term Financial Goals:

_____

_____

_____

_____

_____

How Career and Financial
Goals Fit Into Your Personal Life

One of the keys to being able to achieve goals is to constantly evaluate what your goals are and be ready to modify them as unexpected events happen in your life. At times, things might go better than planned. In some situations, however, you may have to deal with unexpected obstacles. There may also be times when you find that a change in focus will lead to better results.

As you get older, your priorities and values will change. You will become more mature and your outlook on life will be altered as you obtain additional life experience. For these reasons, you always want to keep an open mind as you're confronted with new and exciting opportunities that may require you to alter your goals and objectives.

Over time, you will be forced to make important, potentially life-changing decisions, whether they relate to your career, finances, or personal life. Never make these decisions rashly. Also, don't lose focus on whatever it is you're trying to accomplish in the long term. Always remember that short-term sacrifices may be a necessity, and that there are seldom any shortcuts to achieving success.

Finally, try to choose goals you're truly passionate about and that you believe in. This will help you stay on track over the long term, because you really want to experience the success associated with achieving your goal(s).

Creating a Personalized Goal-Achievement Action Plan

Simply listing your goals in writing and referring to them often (on a daily or weekly basis) is a major step toward being able to achieve those goals. Especially to accomplish your long-term goals. However, you'll need to devise a detailed action plan for each goal as well as a timeline. One of the first steps in achieving your primary long-term goals is to divide each of them up into a series of smaller, more achievable short-term goals, and then to create a timeline for achieving each of those smaller goals.

For example, suppose you have $5,000 in credit card debt, spread over five different credit cards. Your long-term (five year) plan might be to eliminate that debt, but your short-term goals should include reducing the balance owed on each card by a particular amount each month, starting with the card(s) with the highest interest rates. Thus, each month as you pay off some of the outstanding balance owed on your credit cards (not just the minimum interest payment), you'll see your overall debt slowly and systematically decrease.

Once you set out to begin defining and achieving your goals, this becomes an ongoing process that requires commitment, hard work, and dedication on your part. You must focus your energies and then stay focused until your objectives are completed. At times, this won't be an easy process, so one of the challenges you'll face is staying motivated.

The action plan you devise for achieving your goals must be personalized to meet your own needs, lifestyle, and personality. You never want to take on too much, or you'll quickly find yourself overwhelmed and frustrated. Likewise, you always want to be challenged in order to maintain your interest and motivation.

In order to succeed, you'll have to determine, over time, what your personal limits are in terms of what you can handle emotionally and physically, and adjust your action plan accordingly. Most importantly, you must never be afraid to fail!

When it comes to making life-changing decisions and taking steps to improve your career, personal life, or financial well-being, be prepared to make mistakes, but at the same time, always learn from those mistakes and never repeat them. If you make a mistake, don't look at it as a personal failure and get depressed. Instead, consider it a valuable learning experience. Ask yourself: What would I do differently next time? What can be done to fix the situation now that the mistake has been made? What lessons were learned from the mistake? In the future, how can you (and how *will* you) benefit from the knowledge you acquired? What can be done to ensure that a similar mistake never happens again?

While hard work and dedication will play major roles in your ability to achieve long-term success, no matter what your goals are, your attitude and personality will also be integral factors. Finally, always pay attention to yourself and who you are as a person. Never compromise what you believe to be moral and right, simply to make someone else happy or to achieve a goal. There's always a right way and a wrong way of accomplishing something. The wrong way might save you time, money, and maybe even some frustration, but in the long term, always strive to be the best person you can be.

You can make positive things happen for yourself if you're willing to take control over your own finances and your actions. It's within your power to avoid getting too deep in financial trouble. If you're already in a bad situation, with the proper guidance and internal drive, you can vastly improve and/or drastically alter the situation you're currently in.

Overcoming Current Financial Hardships

Virtually everyone, at some point in their life, goes through financial hardship. This could be a result of getting laid off from work, divorce, personal injury, having a business venture fail, poor investment strategies, drastically overspending, and/or abusing credit cards. Whatever the reason, it's important to take control of the situation and begin turning things around before your financial situation gets even worse.

30

It's all too easy to get into deep financial trouble and then simply give up. However, ignoring the problem, not filing tax returns (not paying federal and state income taxes), allowing your mortgage to be foreclosed, allowing your car to be repossessed, or allowing the credit card companies to charge off your accounts, for example, will all have extremely negative repercussions on your financial well-being and credit report for many years to come. Likewise, don't think that simply declaring bankruptcy will be a quick and easy fix to your financial woes. The bankruptcy laws have changed over the past few years, making it more difficult for most people to benefit from this type of drastic action. Before even considering bankruptcy as a potential option, consult with an accountant, financial planner, and/or attorney.

Even if you're not a financial wizard, you can improve your financial situation and learn how to make your paycheck last. Best of all, many of the strategies you can implement to achieve these financial objectives require a minimal time commitment. What *is* required, however, is that once you develop a plan for improving your financial situation, you adhere to that plan as closely as possible.

Understanding Your Financial Woes

Now that you have calculated your net worth and net available cash flow, perhaps you've seen proof of something you've known for a while—financially, you're in trouble. Well, whatever you do, don't panic! Whatever the cause of your financial situation, you'll want to pay careful attention to the strategies in Chapters 2 through 5, as you learn how to:

▶ Control your spending.

▶ Reduce your debt and make better use of your credit.

▶ Deal with unexpected financial disasters.

▶ Learn how to save money in your everyday life.

▶ Discover easy strategies for saving and investing.

After reviewing the financial worksheets you completed earlier in this chapter, answer the following questions:

1. What is the biggest financial obstacle you're currently facing?

_____

_____

_____

_____

_____

_____

_____

2. What needs to change in order to improve your financial situation?

_____

_____

_____

_____

_____

_____

_____

_____

3. What are the primary causes for your financial problems? Check all that apply:

❑ Overspending.

❑ Lack of understanding about finances and how to manage them.

❑ Carelessness.

❑ Employment problems (being laid off or downsized, pay cut, and so on).

❑ Health-related problems.

❑ Unexpected emergencies.

❑ Not adhering to a budget or miscalculating financial needs.

❑ Poor investment decisions/strategies.

❑ Too much debt or poor use of credit.

❑ Living well beyond your means for too long.

❑ The country's bad economy.

❑ Not properly planning for major expenses (retirement, buying a home, purchasing a car, sending your children to college, and so forth).

Other:

_____

_____

_____

_____

_____

_____

4. What's currently keeping you from improving your financial situation?

_____

_____

_____

_____

_____

_____

_____

_____

_____

Once you've considered some of the reasons behind your current financial situation and perhaps given a few minutes worth of thought toward what it will take to improve your situation, it's time to take stock in your own abilities and potential. While reducing your spending, increasing your savings, and implementing proper money-management strategies will help make your current paycheck last, it's also highly worthwhile to develop strategies for earning more money in the months and years to come so that, as your cost of living increases, so will your ability to meet those financial challenges.

Make Every Penny Count: Developing Your Budget

W ho needs a budget anyway? The answer to this question is simple—everyone! Whether you're trying to live on a relatively low income or have multiple millions, developing and maintaining a budget for yourself and your immediate family will help ensure that you maintain the highest quality of life possible, without squandering your money on unnecessary things such as impulse purchases.

This chapter deals with taking control of your financial situation here and now—today. Later, you'll discover how to better save money in your everyday life, better control your debt, prepare for unexpected financial emergencies, and plan for your financial future. But first, it's necessary to get your current financial situation under control.

Determine How and Where Your Money Is Being Spent

In the previous chapter, you determined your monthly take-home income (which is the amount of money left from your paycheck after taxes and other expenses are automatically taken out of your paycheck.) You were also asked to record all of your fixed and flexible monthly expenses. Right now, it's those expenses we're going to focus on.

All of your expenses fall into one of four categories:

1. **Absolutely Necessary**—An expense you must pay in order to live, such as your mortgage (or rent), insurance premiums, food, car payments, medical expenses, utility bills, and so on.

2. **Important (but not critical)**—These are expenses that are not crucial for your everyday survival, but somehow enhance your quality of life. Your cell phone bill and entertainment expenses (movies, cable TV, and so forth) are monthly expenses that may be important to you, but you could live without these things, if absolutely necessary.

3. **Not Critical**—These are expenses that allow you to maintain your current lifestyle or allow you to enjoy various comforts, but are not critical. For example, spending $3.00 every morning on a cup of premium coffee. This adds up to at least $90.00 per month. Another example of a *not critical* expense is driving a luxury car (and making high monthly payments) when you could drive a more practical vehicle with lower payments or that's more fuel efficient (thus saving you money on gas).

4. **Frivolous**—These are expenses that are not at all necessary, such as random shopping sprees or purchases from late-night infomercials. Focus on those random things you buy each and every day that you simply don't need or want. For one week, carry around a pen and paper and write down every time you spend money on something, even if it's a soda, pack of gum, or newspaper. These frivolous expenses add up fast!

Take another look at the Expense Worksheets from the previous chapter (pages 18–20). This time, next to each type of expense, associate it with one of the four expense categories, based on its importance to you. This is the first step toward figuring out how much and where you can begin to trim your expenses in order to save money.

As you categorize each expense, think about its impact on your life and determine how necessary it really is. Also consider what the impact would be if you were able to somehow reduce each type of expense, as opposed to totally eliminating them from your budget. For example, for your cable TV bill, could you keep your cable TV service, but reduce the number of premium channels you subscribe to in order to cut your monthly bill by $10, $20, $30 or more?

Strategies for cutting your everyday expenses without impacting your lifestyle too much will be covered in Chapter 5. But for now, start prioritizing your expenses and thinking about what's truly important to you.

Every penny you cut from your monthly expenses now could ultimately be used to increase your savings, reduce your debt, or assist you in making a large purchase relating to one of your long-term goals (such as buying a car or home). A major strategy for successfully developing a budget that will work for you is to clearly differentiate between your wants and needs.

Prioritizing Your Monthly Expenses Worksheet

Directions: Write the amount of each monthly expense in the appropriate column. Next, consider how much you could deduct from each monthly expense by making some necessary cutbacks. Write your new monthly budget for each expense in the last column on the right ("New Amount to Allocate Each Month"). This is the budget (your targeted expense amount) you'll work with in the future.

Expense Type	Absolutely Necessary Exp.($)	Important Exp.($)	Not Critical Exp. ($)	Frivolous Exp.($)	New Amt. to Allocate Each Month ($)
Alimony/Child Support Payments					
Auto Insurance					
Cable TV Bill					
Car Payment					
Cellular Phone Bill					
Child Care/Babysitting					
Clothing					
Commuting Costs					
Credit Card Payments					
Dining out/Take-out Food Expenses					
#1 TOTALS:					

Expense Type	Absolutely Necessary Exp.($)	Important Exp.($)	Not Critical Exp. ($)	Frivolous Exp.($)	New Amt. to Allocate Each Month ($)
Disability Insurance					
Donations to Charities					
Dues for Organizations, Clubs, and Religious Institutions					
Education					
Electric Bill					
Entertainment/ Recreation Expenses					
Food & Groceries					
Fuel Bill					
Gas Bill					
Gas for Vehicle(s)					
Gifts					
Home Insurance (Renter's Insurance)					
Home Maintenance/ Upkeep Costs					
Internet Connection Fees					
Investment to Stocks, Mutual Funds, etc.					
Laundry/Dry Cleaning					
Life Insurance					
#2 TOTALS:					

Expense Type	Absolutely Necessary Exp.($)	Important Exp.($)	Not Critical Exp. ($)	Frivolous Exp.($)	New Amt. to Allocate Each Month ($)
Medical, Prescriptions, and Dental Expenses					
Medical/Health Insurance					
Newspapers, Magazines, and Books					
Other Loan Payment(s)					
Parking for Your Vehicle(s)					
Payment to Retirement Account(s)					
Payment to Savings for Child's College					
Personal Care & Grooming Products/ Fees					
Pet Supplies and Expenses(Vet, Grooming, Food, etc.)					
Rent/Mortgage					
School/Education- Related Expenses (Textbooks, Tuition, etc.)					
Taxes (Real Estate, etc.)					
Telephone Bill					
Trash Removal					
Vacations					
#3 TOTALS:					

Expense Type	Absolutely Necessary Exp.($)	Important Exp.($)	Not Critical Exp. ($)	Frivolous Exp.($)	New Amt. to Allocate Each Month ($)
Vehicle Maintenance					
Water Bill					
Other Expense: _____					
Other Expense: _____					
Other Expense: _____					
Other Expense: _____					
#4 TOTALS:					
#1 TOTALS:					
#2 TOTALS:					
#3 TOTALS:					
#4 TOTALS:					
GRAND TOTALS:					

Find Ways to Cut Expenses

At the bottom of each column from the Prioritizing Your Monthly Expenses Worksheet, add up the totals. Now, let's take a closer look at those totals:

Absolutely Necessary Monthly Expenses Total: $_____

Important Monthly Expenses Total: $_____

Not Critical Monthly Expenses Total: $_____

Frivolous Monthly Expenses Total: $_____

Either by adding up all of these expenses, or taking the total from the worksheet in Chapter 1, you know what your current monthly expenses are. The total of the far-right column from the Prioritizing Your Monthly Expenses Worksheet should signify your total new monthly budget for expenses, taking into account ways you plan to save money each month. Now, perform the following calculation to determine the potential savings you hope to have each month as a result of your proposed cutbacks:

Total Expenses – "New Amount to Allocate Each Month" Column Total = Savings

Total Expenses: $_____

New Amount to Allocate Each Month: –_____

Savings: $_____

Evaluating Your Expenses

First, let's evaluate your Absolutely Necessary Expenses. Chances are, things such as your mortgage (rent), car payments, and insurance premiums were included. While you can't eliminate these expenses from your budget, you might be able to reduce them. For example, you could potentially refinance your mortgage at a lower interest rate and save several hundred dollars per month. Or, if you're paying rent and drastic money-saving measures need to be taken to cure your financial woes, you could move to a less expensive home or apartment. As for your car payments, you could potentially refinance your car or trade in your vehicle and purchase or lease one that will require lower monthly payments. Even insurance premiums could potentially be reduced if you shop around for the best rates or raise your deductibles. (Warning: Before raising your insurance deductibles, consider the financial consequences if you actually need to make a claim. For example, if you get into a car accident, can you afford to pay a $1,000 deductible to repair your car as opposed to a $250 or $500 deductible?)

Looking at your Important Expenses, carefully evaluate each of them and consider ways you might be able to reduce each of those expenses (not necessarily *eliminate* them). For example, could you do a better job shopping for the best deal for your cell phone service and cut your monthly bill from $65 per month to $30 per month, simply by reducing the number of daytime or anytime minutes you have available to talk on your plan? Chances are you can still get unlimited nights and weekends, plus long-distance calls included at the lower rate.

As you start evaluating your Not Critical Expenses, depending on how much money you want or need to reduce from your overall budget, consider eliminating some or all of these expenses as opposed to reducing them. Once again, consider your priorities and what's truly important to you and your quality of life. Could you cut costs by buying or subscribing to fewer magazines and newspapers each month and visit the library more (or obtain the same information, for free, from the Internet)? Instead of purchasing lavish gifts for friends and family, could you make gifts yourself? When planning your vacation, if you use the Internet-based travel sites, you could often save at least 60 percent off the cost of your travel as opposed to booking your travel directly with an airline or using a travel agent.

Finally, take a look at all of those Frivolous Expenses you have each month. Your best option for these is simply to eliminate them from your budget and teach yourself discipline when it comes to making impulse buying decisions. Just because something you see is on sale, it doesn't mean you absolutely *must* purchase it—no matter how good the deal is. If you don't need the item, don't purchase it! When it comes to reducing your monthly expenses, your Frivolous Expenses should be the very first things to get cut or drastically reduced.

Making Your Money Work Harder for You

If you're like most people, chances are you have a predetermined monthly income. Of course, if you earn commissions or work overtime, you'll earn more, but you can pretty much assume your monthly income will be within a specific range. Because drastically increasing the amount of money that comes in each month isn't an option (at least in the short term), it's important to evaluate your overall budget and determine ways to make the money you have work harder for you.

Chapters 3 and 5 focus on ways to cut your everyday spending and reduce your debt. There are also countless other things you can do to better utilize the money you now have available. Every month, if you save just $100 by doing very simple things, that money you save will add up quickly. (That's $1,200 per year in savings! If invested properly, that $1,200 could be worth a lot more in the not-so-distant future.)

Here are just a few ideas on how to make your money work harder for you:

▶ If you use credit cards, apply for cards with the lowest possible fees and interest rates and then transfer your outstanding balances from higher interest rate cards.

▶ Immediately work toward reducing your credit card balances so you're not paying so much interest per month. Likewise, consider refinancing your home and/or car to reduce the amount of interest you're paying.

▶ When choosing a bank, select one that pays the highest interest rates for money in savings accounts, plus has the lowest fees to maintain a checking account. In some situations, you'll find that a credit union offers the best rates. Shop around for the best deals.

▶ If you have a significant amount of money sitting in a low interest earning savings account, consider putting those discretionary funds into some type of investment, such as mutual funds. While you may incur some additional financial risk, the financial rewards could be worthwhile. Be sure to consult with a financial advisor and do your research before making any type of financial investment, plus be sure to diversify your investments. (Don't invest in a single stock or mutual fund, for example.)

▶ Find ways to reduce your utility expenses. For example, throughout your home, use more energy efficient (and/or lower wattage) lightbulbs and turn down the airconditioning or heat during the day when you're at work. When purchasing major appliances, pay attention to their energy efficiency rating and look for the Energy Star label (*www.energystar.gov*). Energy Star is a government-backed program helping businesses and individuals protect the environment by promoting better energy efficiency. The Department of Energy Efficiency offers free information at *www.eere.energy.gov/consumerinfo/energy_savers*. This information is also available by calling 1-800-DOE-EREC.

Strategies for Sticking to Your Budget

Once you set a budget for yourself, it's important to stick with it. Sorry, those impulse shopping sprees need to stop. Hopefully, you've already begun to discover ways you can immediately reduce your monthly expenses. As you decide what expense-cutting strategies you'll utilize, consider the following:

▶ Why are you implementing each expense-cutting strategy? What's your specific goal or objective?

▶ What will the benefit be (short-term and long-term) of each strategy?

▶ What will the immediate impact be on you and your lifestyle?

▶ What do you anticipate the financial outcome will be after implementing each cost-cutting strategy?

44

Next, as you implement each strategy, focus on your objectives and evaluate the results on an ongoing basis. After implementing cost cutting strategies and a budget, the biggest challenge will be sticking to it and allowing it to work for you. Choosing ways to save money or creating a budget is only the first step. Now, you must adjust your lifestyle and adhere to the cost-cutting measures you've selected and make a conscious effort *not* to deviate from the budget you create.

Your personal motivation will be one of the key factors that will help you stick to the budget you create, plus adhere to the expense-cutting and money-saving strategies you implement. Your motivation should be driven by your long-term goals. For example, if your goal is to save enough money to buy a home or condo in five years, fixate your mind on that objective and force yourself to do what's necessary to achieve that goal. Dedication and discipline are critical! To help, obtain a photograph of your dream home, for example, and display it prominently on your desk at work or on your nightstand at home. If you're saving up to purchase a nicer car in two to four years, go to your local toy store and purchase the Matchbox car version of your dream car, and keep that toy visible on your desk.

Figure out what motivates you and then do what's necessary to stay focused and on track when adhering to your newly developed budget. For some people, developing a reward system also helps. For example, every month, if you save a predetermined amount of money, treat yourself to a night out or dinner at your favorite restaurant. Or, if you know you're saving $90 per month by drinking nonpremium coffee or because you quit smoking, use that money saved to purchase something you really want at the end of each month or quarter.

Don't allow yourself to justify reasons for straying from your budget. At the end of each month, each quarter, and each year, evaluate your progress. This alone should help keep you motivated as you see yourself getting closer and closer to achieving your long-term goals. Develop an ongoing series of well-thought-out financial and budgeting strategies for achieving your financial goals. Implementing a random strategy here and there and not being consistent will not allow you to achieve long-term success.

Balance Your Checkbook Monthly

There are two important reasons for a budget conscious person to balance (or reconcile) their checkbook on the regular basis. First, doing this allows you to keep careful track of how much money is available in your checking account. Second, it helps avoid costly errors. If, for example, you forget to take into account bank fees, or forget you made an ATM withdrawal, you could accidentally bounce a check due to insufficient funds. Not only can this be embarrassing, but it can be costly, because you'll be forced to pay additional fees that someone on a tight budget should definitely avoid.

As you take control of your personal budget and spending, start by balancing your checkbook, especially if you're watching every penny. To pay bills and cover living expenses, the average person writes at least 240 checks per year. In addition, a growing number of people are using their debit card or online banking to pay bills using funds from their checking account, without actually having to write a check.

When you write a check, the money is taken from your checking account. In addition, money gets removed from your account when you use a debit card, withdraw from an ATM (automatic teller machine), pay a bill using check-by-phone or automatic payment options, and pay related banking fees. Especially if you're on a tight budget, it's important to have ongoing knowledge of exactly how much money is available within your checking account in order to avoid accidentally bouncing checks and incurring additional fees from the bank.

Balancing (or reconciling) your checkbook requires a minimal time commitment and little mathematical skill. Furthermore, you can use a calculator, computer, or PDA to make the process even easier. This process should be done every month when you receive your checking-account statement from your bank. If you use online banking, access you account on an ongoing basis, because you'll be able to see exactly when deposits and checks clear.

Follow these easy steps to balance your checkbook:

1. Keep an ongoing record of all transactions relating to your checking account as they happen. It's too easy to forget making a transaction if you don't write it down immediately. When recording a transaction, write down the date, type of transaction, the amount of money associated with the transaction, plus any additional notes. All of this information can be recorded in your checkbook register (provided with your checks) or using your computer, with a program such as Microsoft Money or Intuit Quicken. If you have access to the Internet, there's a free checkbook balancing application that you can dowload at *www.xfcu.org/Money/checking_balance.html*.

You'll want to keep track of:

‣ All transactions made using a bank teller.

‣ ATM transactions.

‣ Bank fees.

‣ Checks that are written.

‣ All deposits (direct deposits, ATM deposits, teller deposits).

‣ Online banking transactions.

‣ Purchases made with your debit card.

‣ Recurring automatic payments.

‣ Transfers of money between your accounts.

Your checkbook register will probably look something like this:

Check Number	Date	Transaction Description	Payment/ Debit (-)	Code	Fee (-)	Deposit/ Credit (+)	TotalFor Transaction

Note: In the Code column of your check register, you can enter the type of transaction. Use this list to make it easier:

D = Deposit.

DP = Debit Card Purchase.

ATM = Cash Withdrawal.

AP = Automatic Payment.

FT = Fund Transfer.

I = Interest Earned.

SC = Service Charge or Bank Fee.

TD = Tax Deductible.

2. As soon as your monthly bank statement arrives, compare all of the transactions you recorded in your check register with the transactions listed on your statement. Each time you see a match, place a checkmark next to that entry in your check register and on the bank statement. Use a pencil, in case you need to correct an error.

3. In a perfect world, the balance on your statement should match the balance in your checkbook register for the date the statement was printed by the bank. In reality, however, this rarely happens. There will most likely be transactions listed in your check register, such as uncleared checks, that aren't yet listed on your bank statement. Likewise, there may be banking fees on your statement that you forgot to list in your check register. To deal with this, subtract from your bank statement's total balance any checks, debit transactions, fees, and service charges, for example, that are listed in your register but not listed on your bank statement. Next, add to the bank statement's total balance any deposits that are listed in your check register but not included on the statement. This adjusted bank statement balance should now be identical to your checkbook register's balance.

4. Look for common errors. If, after making the necessary adjustments, the total listed on your bank statement does not match your check register (for the date the bank statement was issued), determine if any outstanding checks cleared, for example, perhaps from two or three months ago. Also, recheck all of your mathematical calculations and make sure you didn't transpose any numbers. Make sure you remembered to calculate in all of the various banking fees.

To make balancing your checkbook a bit easier, complete these two worksheets each month, then perform the following calculations:

Worksheet #1—Outstanding Checks

(List any checks you wrote that have *not yet been included* on your bank statement. Be sure to list any other debit card transactions and transactions involving money being taken out of your checking account that don't yet appear on the bank statement. Note: List banking fees separately.)

Check Number or Transaction Description	Amount

TOTAL: $_____

Worksheet #2—Outstanding Deposits

(List any deposits or transactions involving money put into your checking account that *are not listed* on your bank statement.)

Deposit or Transaction Description	Amount

TOTAL: $_____

Once these two worksheets are complete, perform this calculation:

	Ending Balance on Your Bank Statement	$_____
ADD (+)	Total Outstanding Deposits (Total From Preceding Worksheet #2)	$_____
SUBTRACT (-)	Total Outstanding Checks (Total From Preceding Worksheet #1)	$_____
SUBTRACT (-)	All Banking Fees	$_____
ADD (+)	Interest Earned (if applicable)	$_____

NEW BALANCE: $_____

(Your New Balance should be equal to the balance listed in your check register.)

Who Can Afford to Save?

Ideally, it's an excellent strategy to have enough money in savings to support yourself financially for at least three months if, for some reason, you can't work and earn an income. In addition to saving for your retirement and other long-term expenses, putting money aside each month into a separate savings account will help you plan for an unexpected emergency or allow you to have the funds available if there is something you want to purchase that isn't calculated into your budget.

Depending on what your goals are, there are many ways to find money within your monthly budget that can be saved instead of spent. For example, on your nightstand, keep a jar for loose change. At the end of each month, deposit that jar of coins into a separate savings account. If you're like most people, you'll wind up collecting $25 to $100 (or more) in loose change every month.

The best way to start saving, however, is to automatically take a percentage (say 20 to 30 percent) of your discretionary income—the money from your paycheck that's left over after you pay *all* of your expenses—and put it immediately into savings each month. Use this formula:

Step 1   **Take-Home Income – All Expenses
= Your Discretionary Income**

Step 2   **Your Discretionary Income x .20 (or .30)
= Amount To Be Saved**

Right now, you might not have any leftover disposable income (discretionary income). Hence, you have no money to put into savings. Your first task is to implement your budget. This will allow you to systematically begin cutting expenses and reducing your debt. Once you begin incorporating these strategies, if done correctly, you should begin to see your discretionary income increase. To help this figure increase even more, consider implementing some of the strategies described in Chapters 3 and 5.

Discretionary Income: Make the Right Decisions

Your discretionary income is the money you have left over after your expenses are paid each month. It's called discretionary income because you can decide exactly what to do with it. How you spend, save, invest, or utilize your discretionary income is potentially your key to getting yourself out of debt and achieving your long-term financial goals. With the money left over after all of your expenses are paid, you could:

51

▸ Spend it on frivolous things. This is what most people tend to do. As a result, they often remain in debt, aren't able to save any money, and sometimes overspend. If you're debt-free, however, and have a comfortable level of savings, spending frivolously on occasion is certainly within your right and can be highly enjoyable.

▸ Put some or all of your discretionary income into savings or investments (allowing that money to grow) and plan for the future. If you invest just $100 per month into a mutual fund, for example, over time, you'll see that investment grow significantly.

▸ Use it to reduce your debt. For example, pay off credit card balances or student loans. You could also pay extra toward your mortgage or pay off your car loan faster. By paying off your debt, you'll ultimately be saving all of that money you're currently paying in interest charges and other fees. At the same time, you'll improve your credit rating and ultimately enhance your financial stability.

Make Your Financial Life Easier: Use Personal Financial Software

Developing and maintaining a budget, tracking expenses, and managing all of your personal or family finances becomes much easier when you use a popular software package, such as Microsoft Money or Intuit Quicken. If you use one of these programs on an ongoing basis, you'll spend much less time actually managing your finances, plus you'll make fewer errors as a result of incorrect mathematical calculations. In addition, these programs are designed to integrate seamlessly with the online banking services offered by many banks and financial institutions, so data from your accounts can automatically be downloaded into the financial software.

Whether you're trying to organize your finances (gather all of your financial information in one place), balance your checkbook, track your spending, reduce your debt, pay your bills, manage investments, or create and implement a budget, one of these programs is an ideal tool for helping to improve your financial situation.

The programs described in this section are Windows-based. Using colorful graphics and easy-to-understand screens, they are easy to set up and use.

Don't worry, there are no cumbersome manuals to read and understand. Everything you need to know is explained on the screen, using each program's help features and informational pop-up windows.

Whether you choose to utilize computer technology to manage your finances or opt to rely on pen, paper, and a calculator, it's important to develop a thorough understanding of your personal financial situation, focus carefully on how you're spending your money, and then choose the appropriate strategies to help make your paycheck last based on your own personal situation and objectives.

➤ Microsoft Money 2004 (or Later)

Company:	Microsoft Corporation
Phone:	Contact your local software retailer
Website:	*www.microsoft.com/money*
Price:	$24.95–$74.95 (depending on version and ongoing rebate offers)

If you already use any of the programs in the Microsoft Office Suite, chances are you'll already be familiar with the basic operation of Microsoft Money 2004 (or later). Updated annually, Microsoft Money 2004 is the 12th edition of this popular financial software package to be released. The standard version ($24.95) allows you to organize your personal finances, create a budget, develop a plan for reducing your debt, balance your checkbook, and pay your bills (either traditionally by writing checks or via online banking). Microsoft Money 2004 Deluxe ($44.95) offers all of the features of the standard edition, plus a handful of useful tools for managing your investments. Microsoft Money 2004 Suite ($74.95) also adds a handful of additional tools for managing taxes and handling financial-related legal issues.

For most people first starting to manage their finances using a computer, the standard or deluxe version of Microsoft Money is more than adequate. What's great about this package is that you can use one module at a time. For example, the software can be used simply to track expenses or balance your checkbook. Then, as you need the additional functionality, it's available to you. This program is perfect for someone who is not at all financially savvy, but has a general knowledge of how to use Windows-based programs.

➤ Quicken 2004 (or Later)

Company:	Intuit Inc.
Phone:	Contact your local software retailer
Website:	*www.quicken.com*
Price:	$29.95–$79.95 (depending on version)

For almost 20 years, Intuit has been releasing annual editions of Intuit Quicken for Windows-based computers, and with each new version, the program becomes easier to use and more functional. Like Microsoft Money, the latest versions have focused on enhancing the user's ability to utilize online banking services and manage their investments online. The company reports that Intuit Quicken now connects seamlessly with more than 2,000 banks, credit card companies, investment companies, and 401(k) providers via the Internet. This means that there's often no need to enter all of your financial data, because the information can be downloaded. When it comes to financial programs, Intuit Quicken is the most popular package on the market, with more than 15 million active users worldwide.

Depending on your needs, several versions of this software are available. Intuit Quicken 2004 Basic ($29.95) is the perfect tool for anyone looking to begin managing their finances using a computer. The program offers modules that allow you to easily balance your checkbook, pay bills, and track spending. Intuit Quicken 2004 Deluxe ($59.95) adds tools for preparing your taxes and monitoring investments. Other versions available include Intuit Quicken 2004 Premier and Quicken 2004 Premier Home & Business.

As you use any version, the "big picture" financial questions the software will help you answer are: "What do I have?", "How am I doing?", "How can I do better?", and "What actions need to be taken to achieve my goals?" Because the program is so easy to use, you'll be able to set it up and begin benefiting from its functionality within minutes. Throughout the year, you'll easily be able to manage not only your money, but your investments and tax-related information. The software will also remind you to pay specific bills on time (either traditionally or using online banking), ensuring that you don't incur late fees or penalties.

In addition to the software, Inuit also supports the Quicken.com Website (*www.quicken.com*), which offers a wide range of free financial tools, information, and services to everyone, not just users of the Quicken software.

➤ ExpensAble 6

        Company: One Mind Connect, Inc.

        Phone: 1-949-640-0701

        Website: *www.onemindconnect.com*

        Price: $79.95 (Single User Version)

Unlike Microsoft Money or Intuit Quicken, One Mind Connect ExpensAble is a software package with one objective—to help people track their expenses. Originally designed for business people, this program is extremely easy to use and is ideal for someone first developing their budget and who needs to determine and track exactly how and where they're spending their money. This software allows you to track cash expenditures, checks, credit cards, debit cards, and so on, and quickly categorize your expenses. Each expense, for example, takes just seconds to enter. One Mind Connect ExpensAble can also be integrated easily with Intuit Quicken, so you can transfer all of your expense information without having to reenter data.

Budget Management "On the Go"

Most people don't just sit at home and spend their money. They're typically out and about, shopping at malls, dining at restaurants, and running around town doing errands. Thus, when it comes time to track expenses (and not forgetting about any of them), one way to do this is to write everything down, using a pen and paper, as you incur each expense. Later, when you get home, you can transfer the information into your financial software or budget worksheets. An alternative, however, is to take advantage of the power, convenience, and ease of use of a personal digital assistant (PDA).

The variety of PDAs from PalmOne (*www.palm.com*) or Handspring (*www.handspring.com*), for example, range in price from less than $100 to about $600. These units offer a wide range of computer-like capabilities, but fit in the palm of your hand. Using optional add-on software, much of the functionality and financial management capabilities you'd find in a program such as Microsoft Money, Intuit Quicken, or One Mind Connect ExpensAble, are available to you anytime, anywhere.

You can use a PDA (with optional software) to manage your budget, track expenses, manage your investment portfolio, and so on, plus you can easily transfer your financial data between your PDA and desktop computer with the touch of a single button. For PDAs that operate using Palm OS (operating system), there are dozens of personal finance software packages available.

Because these units can be carried with you, a PDA can become an indispensable personal productivity tool, not just for managing your money, but also for managing your contacts, daily schedule, and a wealth of other information.

The following are a few of the more powerful, yet easy-to-use options ideal for someone first establishing their budget and starting to make a conscious effort to better manage their money. Before purchasing any of these PDA programs, you can download a free trial version from the company's Website. To find additional Palm OS-compatible personal finance programs, visit one of these two Websites and do a search:

▶ The PalmOne Website (*www.palm.com/software*).

▶ PalmGear (*www.palmgear.com*).

➤ Personal Money Tracker 7.8.6 (or Later)
    Company: Joan McBride
    Phone: Not Applicable—Software must be
                 downloaded
    Website: *www.palmgear.com/software*
              (do a search for "Personal Money Tracker 7.8.6")
    Price: $19.95

This program is designed to help you manage all aspects of your personal finances using your Palm PDA. It's a powerful, yet inexpensive and easy-to-use program that offers a wide range of features for tracking income and expenses. There's even a programmable alarm feature to remind you to pay individual bills on specific dates.

➤ Pocket Quicken 2.0x
    Company: LandWare, Inc.
    Phone: 1-201-261-7944
    Website: *www.landware.com*
    Price: $39.95

Based on the Windows version of Intuit Quicken, this PDA version has been scaled down, but still offers users who are on the go the ability to quickly and easily manage and organize their finances. Using this program with your PDA, you can enter expenses as they're incurred, plus oversee your budget anytime and anywhere. This will help you stick to your predefined spending plan, plus allow you to keep all of your account balances at your fingertips. Using LandWare Pocket Quicken, you can manage your savings and checking accounts, credit cards, debit cards, track ATM usage, and even oversee your investment portfolio.

This program is powerful enough to use on its own, or you can quickly and easily transfer data between LandWare Pocket Quicken and any version of Intuit Quicken for your desktop computer.

➤ SplashMoney 2.7x

    Company: SplashData, Inc.

    Phone: Not Applicable—Software must be downloaded

    Website: *www.splashdata.com*

    Price: $14.95

This extremely inexpensive program offers expense tracking capabilities while on the go. You can record and manage information about multiple accounts at once to help keep track of your credit cards, checking account(s), ATM/debit card(s), and cash. You can then display individual balances for each account, or display a customized report featuring an overview of your entire financial situation.

Reduce Debt to Make Your Paycheck Last

This chapter focused primarily on taking control of your expenses and finding ways to reduce those unnecessary monthly expenses that are eating away at your paycheck. The more money you can subtract from your expenses and add to your discretionary income, the better off you'll be financially. The next chapter focuses on reducing your debt, managing credit, and making the best use of the credit you have available.

Managing, Reducing, and Ultimately Eliminating Debt

For financial institutions such as Citigroup, MBNA America, Bank One, Chase, Capital One, Providian, Bank of America, Household Bank, and Fleet, issuing credit cards to consumers is a very profitable part of their business. In fact, in 2001, the global sales volume for Visa, MasterCard, and American Express was $2.1 trillion, $986 billion, and $298 billion respectively (as reported by CardWeb.com).

CardWeb.com (*www.cardweb.com*) is a leading online publisher of information pertaining to all types of payment cards, including, but not limited to, credit cards, debit cards, smart cards, prepaid cards, ATM cards, loyalty cards, and phone cards. This organization also reported that the average U.S. household has a current average total outstanding credit card balance of about $8400. In March 2002, the 185 million Americans with credit cards owed about $660 billion on them, and that figure has been increasing steadily.

For the consumer who relies on credit cards and carries a significant balance, interest charges, annual fees, late fees, over limit fees, and other charges from the credit card issuers can be significant. It's often these fees and charges that contribute to people getting into debt and not being able to easily remedy the situation.

Unfortunately, the credit card companies make it easy to apply for and often obtain credit cards, especially if your credit rating is average or better. In a typical year, credit card companies mail more than 5 billion applications and offers to approximately 200 million people in America alone. Thus, the average American adult receives at least one credit card offer per week.

By using incentives, rewards, the knowledge that many people with financial problems will rely on their credit cards to pay their everyday living expenses, and by capitalizing on people's lack of understanding of how credit actually works, credit cards generate huge profits for financial institutions, while many consumers are getting themselves deeper and deeper into debt.

Sure, credit cards are convenient and, in some situations, beneficial to the consumer, but only if they're used correctly. Part of successfully utilizing credit cards involves taking steps to shop around for the best deals and offers.

Of course, credit cards aren't the only type of debt people accrue. Banks and financial institutions offer mortgages, second mortgages, home equity loans, personal lines of credit, and a wide range of other opportunities to borrow money and pay it off over time, with interest.

This chapter will help you better understand credit and how it can help you or hurt you, depending on how you use (or abuse) it. Developing a good credit rating is critical in today's society. Taking advantage of the credit you're given is also perfectly acceptable, assuming you use it responsibly. If, like so many other people, you've already gotten yourself into some trouble by relying too much on your credit or by racking up extremely high balances on your credit cards, it's important to immediately change your spending and credit-use behavior. Begin developing a plan to reduce and eventually eliminate the debt you've already acquired. Once you acquire massive credit card debt, the interest charges, late fees, over limit fees, and so on, keep adding up, month after month, until those balances are paid off (or settled), whether or not you continue to use your credit cards. It's in your best interest, financially, to reduce and eventually eliminate your high interest debt as quickly as possible.

Calculating Your Debt

In this section, begin by adding up all of your current debt in order to better evaluate the situation you're in right now and begin developing a plan to reduce and eventually eliminate this debt. Every month, your goal should be to pay off at least a small portion of your outstanding debt, without incurring new debt. Only by doing this will you break out of the cycle of racking up new debt and paying ongoing interest, month after month and year after year.

Long-Term Debt Worksheet

Loan Type	Annual Percentage Rate, or APR (%)	Term (Years)	Fee(s)	Monthly Payment ($)	Outstanding Balance ($)
Mortgage					
Second Mortgage					
Home Equity Loan(s)					
Personal Loan(s)					
Auto Loan(s)					
Student Loan(s)					

TOTAL: $ _____ $ _____

Credit Card Debt Worksheet

Take an inventory of all the credit cards you have right now. To complete the following worksheet, you may need to contact the various credit card issuers to obtain your Annual Percentage Rate (APR) and current balances. This information will also appear on your monthly statement. Be sure to list all of your different Visa, MasterCard, Discover, Diner's Club, and American Express cards, plus your store credit cards and gas station credit cards. To ensure that you don't forget any cards, you might want to compare the list you compile here with what's listed on your credit report, obtained from Experian, Trans Union, or Equifax. (See the section later in this chapter, called "Understanding Your Credit Rating/Credit Score," to learn more about these credit reporting agencies and your credit report.)

Credit Card Name/ Account Number	Phone Number	Annual Fee(s) ($)	APR (%)	Other Fees/ Charges ($)	Credit Limit ($)	Monthly Payment ($)	Current Balance ($)

TOTAL: $_____ $_____

Strategies for Reducing Your Debt

Your ability to lower your long-term debt will rely on several factors, including:

▸ Your current credit rating/credit score—People with the best credit are always given the lowest interest rates and best loan options.

▸ Your ability to make additional payments and/or pay off long-term debt (such as your mortgage or car loan) early—Doing this will lower the balances of your loans and, in the long term, save you significant money in interest payments, and so on.

▸ Your willingness and ability to refinance your loan(s) at better rates and/or for shorter terms—With interest rates for mortgages constantly changing, you might be able to save hundreds of dollars per month—thousands over the term of the loan—if you refinance at a lower interest rate and/or for a shorter term. Whether you're looking to refinance a mortgage or a car loan, for example, contact at least three reputable financial institutions to see what interest rates and loan(s) you qualify for and then use a mortgage calculator, for example, to determine if you'll be able to save money. Make sure you take into account any fees, closing costs, points, and so forth, that may be involved in refinancing your long-term loan(s). The more time you invest in finding the best deals, the more money you'll ultimately save. Lowering your loan's interest rate just one quarter of one percentage point, for example, can make a tremendous difference over a 15, 20, or 30 year period for a mortgage. Keep in mind, however, that if you've already damaged your credit rating, refinancing your mortgage or car loans will be significantly more difficult and you will not be able to obtain the most competitive rates. Companies that claim to offer credit to consumers "regardless of their credit history" are usually either flat-out scams or charge very high interest rates and fees.

There are several things you can do to immediately reduce and take control of your credit card debt, especially if your credit rating is at least average. Some of your options include:

▸ Find and apply for better deals on credit cards (in terms of lower APRs, annual fees, and so on), then transfer your existing balances from the high interest cards to the lower interest cards. The section of this chapter called "Find the Best Credit Card Deals," will help you shop around for the best credit card offers. Once you transfer your balances, close the accounts with the high interest rates when those balances reach zero. The goal isn't to acquire more credit cards, but to reduce what you're paying in interest and fees on your existing debt.

▸ If your outstanding credit card debt is extremely high and spread over multiple cards (all of which are maxed out, or close to it), you might consider a consolidation loan. This is one loan (typically available at a much lower interest rate than your credit cards) that will allow you to pay off your multiple credit cards in full and then pay off just one loan over time. It's easy to obtain this type of loan if you already own a home or have average or above average credit.

▸ To reduce your credit card debt on a monthly basis, pay at least a little more than the minimum required payment listed on your credit card statement. That minimum payment covers the interest charges and fees related to the credit card. Only a very small portion (if any) of the minimum payment typically gets applied to the principal you actually owe. To reduce your debt, you need to be lowering your principal (the balance of what you owe) on an ongoing basis, not just pay the related interest charges and fees. Even paying $10 to $50 above the minimum payment each month will be beneficial to you in terms of reducing your debt and improving your long-term financial situation. To protect your credit rating, you always want to pay at least the minimum payment due on each credit card. Don't just ignore incoming bills and monthly statements that you can't afford to pay. When you're late on payments, the credit issuers will start making non-stop collection calls to your home and possibly your place of work, and they will also send countless collection letters until they're paid. They'll also report your delinquency to the credit bureaus, which will reflect negatively on your credit report.

▶ If your credit card situation is out of control and you simply can't afford even to make the minimum monthly payments, consider negotiating a settlement (or payment plan) with each credit card company as soon as possible. When you settle with a credit card company, your credit card account(s) will be closed and each settlement will be reported to the credit reporting agencies (Equifax, Experian, and Trans Union) as a settlement (as opposed to a charge-off). Each settlement will damage your credit rating and stay on your credit report for up to seven years, but you'll often be able to settle for between 40% and 60% of what you actually owe and/or set up an installment plan for paying off the debt, while stopping interest and late fees from adding up. While a settlement doesn't look good on your credit report, a charge-off (where the balance is unpaid and written off by the credit issuer) is much worse for your credit rating. It's important that you take control of the situation and try to work with the credit card companies in good faith before your account goes into collection or gets charged off. Even after a charge-off takes place, you could get sued for the full balance you owe, plus all fees, and so forth.

▶ To maintain your good credit, ideally you should carry a balance that's equal to no more than half of your credit limit on each card. You'll also want to pay more than the minimum amount due each month. Ideally, you should maintain a zero balance on your credit cards by using them, but then paying the bill in full, when you receive your monthly statement. This allows you to enjoy the convenience of using a credit card, without incurring any interest charges.

Understanding Your Credit Rating/Credit Score

Your credit report is a document compiled by three different credit bureaus—Equifax, Experian, and Trans Union. It contains detailed information about you, including your social security number, address, where you work, and your bill payment history. This report also shows if you've been arrested or have filed for bankruptcy. Companies that issue credit, such as credit card companies, mortgage companies, and other businesses have access to your credit report and use this information to determine whether or not you are creditworthy. Companies that have already issued you credit or loans report monthly to the credit bureaus about whether or not you pay your bills on time and as promised. Negative information about your payment history can stay on your credit report for up to seven years. Information about bankruptcies can remain on your credit report for 10 years, while details about any criminal activity (such as arrests and convictions) can stay on your credit report indefinitely.

In addition to simply listing all of your creditors, the credit bureaus also calculate a credit score (also called FICO score) that is part of your credit report. To calculate your credit score, information about your bill-paying history, the number and type of accounts you have, late payments, collection actions, outstanding debt, and the age of your accounts are all taken into account. Your credit score is a primary indicator, used to predict how creditworthy you are. Credit scores range between 300 and 850. The higher your score, the better your credit rating is.

According to Equifax, FICO scores among U.S. consumers are distributed as follows:

20% of consumers are above	780	These people have the best credit rating.
20% of consumers are in the range	745–780	
20% of consumers are in the range	690–745	
20% of consumers are in the range	620–690	
20% of consumers are below	619	These people will find it difficult, if not impossible, to obtain new credit cards, a mortgage, or a car loan. They are considered extremely high credit risks.

Obtaining Your Credit Report and FICO Credit Score

Every six months, it's an excellent idea to review your credit report from all three credit bureaus. This will help you determine your creditworthiness, plus allow you to identify any errors on your credit reports. You can obtain your credit report online (within minutes) by purchasing a copy of it. You can, however, obtain a free copy of your credit report if you are denied credit as a result of information on one or more credit reports. By mailing a letter (containing your request along with your name, address, phone number, Social Security number, and date of birth) to each credit bureau, you can also purchase a printed copy of your credit report for $9.00 per copy.

The addresses and phone numbers for the three credit bureaus are:

Equifax
   PO Box 740241
   Atlanta, GA 30374-0241
   Phone: 1-800-685-1111
   www.econsumer.equifax.com/webapp/ConsumerProducts/index.jsp

Experian (TRW)
   PO Box 2002
   Allen, TX 75013
   Phone: 1-888-EXPERIAN
   www.experian.com

Trans Union
   PO Box 1000
   Chester, PA 19022
   Phone: 1-900-916-8800
   www.transunion.com

For a monthly or annual fee (or a one-time fee per report), you can obtain copies of your credit report and credit score online and subscribe to monitoring services that will notify you as changes, updates, or inquiries are made to your credit report. Many of these services also make it easier to correct errors on your reports. Such services are offered online by all three credit bureaus. For about $30, you can also obtain a 3-in-1 credit report, which combines information from all three credit bureaus into one report.

To save time, you should obtain your credit reports online (which takes minutes) as opposed to requesting the reports by mail, which can take as long as 30 days.

If you're planning to purchase a home, buy a car (or other big ticket item using credit), or apply for any type of credit or loan, it's an excellent idea to review your credit report and develop an understanding of your credit score in order to determine whether or not you will qualify.

There are many things you can do to improve your credit score over time such as:

▶ Pay your monthly bills (credit cards, mortgage, car loan, and so on) on time, for at least six months in a row.

▶ Reduce the balances of your existing credit cards and loans.

▶ Consolidate your credit card balances.

▶ Pay off past due and uncollected debts, such as charge-offs or bills that have been forwarded to collection agencies.

▶ Establish (or reestablish) your credit by obtaining one or more secured credit cards and using them responsibly.

▶ Have a cosigner who has good credit apply for a credit card, car loan, or mortgage with you.

▶ Correct any errors on your credit reports.

▶ Seek out assistance from a legitimate credit counseling or credit consolidation service. For example, the Consumer Credit Counseling Service (CCCS) is a nonprofit organization that offers free or low-cost financial counseling to help families solve their financial problems. CCCS can help you analyze your situation and work with you to develop solutions. There are more than 1,200 CCCS offices in the United States. Call 1-800-388-2227 or visit their Website at *www.cccsatl.org*.

Credit Cards, Secured Credit Cards, and Debit Cards

There are major differences between credit cards (Visa, MasterCard, and so on), secured credit cards, and debit cards. Here is a description of each and a brief explanation about how each works:

▶ **Credit Card**—A credit card, such as a Visa or MasterCard, allows you to pay your balance through monthly installments and/or a revolving line of credit, with the preset spending limit set by the credit card issuer. Your monthly payment can range from a minimum amount, set by your bank, to your entire outstanding balance. As a general rule, if you pay the entire credit card bill at the end of the month, you will be charged no interest. When you maintain a balance, however, the interest you are charged will be at a predetermined Annual Percentage Rate (APR). The APR of every credit card is different. This rate determines how much you'll actually pay each year for the privilege of having credit and for maintaining a balance.

▶ **Secured Credit Card**—This type of credit card is ideal for someone first trying to establish (or reestablish) credit. Virtually anyone who is over the age of 18 and has a valid Social Security number can qualify for a secured credit card. This type of card offers many of the privileges of a regular credit card, however, your credit limit is determined by the amount of money you keep in a separate savings account with the financial institution that issues the card. This savings account acts as insurance for the credit card issuer, in case you default on your payments. The minimum initial deposit is usually $200 (or more), and the fees associated with obtaining a secured credit card tend to be higher than the fees associated with a traditional credit card. There's often a required annual fee, one-time application fee, plus processing fees. On your actual credit report, however, there's no difference between a secured credit card and a regular credit card.

▶ **Debit Card**—This type of card is linked directly to your savings, checking, money market, or mutual fund account. For making purchases, debit cards are accepted wherever Visa or MasterCard are accepted, and the amount of your purchases is immediately deducted directly from your checking, savings, or mutual fund account. In other words, a debit card works just like a paperless check. These cards also work as ATM cards for handling your regular bank transactions, such as making deposits or checking your balances. You're not actually using credit when utilizing a debit card to make a purchase, because the funds are instantly taken from your account.

Find the Best Credit Card Deals

There are literally hundreds of financial institutions that offer credit cards to consumers. To ultimately make the most of your credit and save money in fees and interest, shop around for the best deals. The following are some of the things to consider when evaluating a credit card offer:

▶ **Perks and Rewards**—Depending on the offer, you may receive anything from cash back (rebates) on your purchases to frequent flier miles for your favorite airline, simply for using the credit card. Credit cards with special perks or rewards typically charge an annual fee. Other benefits associated with some credit cards include discounts on certain products and services, insurance, and credit protection. As you'll see, what's offered varies greatly between card issuers. Bank One, for example, offers a credit card associated with the ASPCA. According to Bank One, "As an animal lover, you're committed to extending humane treatment to all creatures, great and small....Each time you use your ASPCA Platinum Visa card, Bank One will donate 1/2% to The ASPCA—at no extra cost to you." Bank One also offers a special credit card to Borders bookstore customers. According to Bank One, "...after your first purchase, you will receive a $20 Gift Card redeemable at any Borders store or online." From then on, you will earn one point for each dollar charged to the card and can redeem the points for Borders merchandise. Purchases made at Borders award two points for each dollar you spend. "Each time you collect 500 points, you will receive a Borders store Reward Certificate worth $5."

▶ **Annual Fee**—This is a fee you pay once per year for the privilege of having that specific credit card. Some card issuers call this a membership or participation fee, and it can vary anywhere from $15 to $150 per year. To be competitive, many credit card issuers charge no annual fee. The fees typically run significantly higher for people with poor credit or those applying for a secured credit card.

▶ **Application Fee**—This is a one-time fee for filling out the application for the credit card and having that application processed. You may be charged this fee whether or not you are accepted and issued a credit card. There are many credit card issuers that charge no application fees. The application fee may be in addition to the card's annual fee. In some cases, you may also be charged a one-time or monthly *processing fee*.

▶ **APR (%)**—This is the Annual Percentage Rate of interest you'll be charged. This represents how much credit will cost you on a yearly basis. The predetermined percentage that the credit card company must disclose to you. In addition to the APR, make sure you pay attention to the *periodic rate* associated with the credit card. This is the rate the card issuer applies to your outstanding balance to calculate your finance charges for each billing period. Also, pay attention to how the credit card issuer computes the balances for purchases.

▶ **Balance Transfer Opportunities**—When applying for a new credit card, some issuers will offer you an extra low APR for a predetermined period, if you transfer balances from your other credit cards to this new account. This can be a way you can save money on interest payments, but make sure you read the fine print and understand the deal being offered before accepting it. After the predetermined period, the APR on your outstanding balance could jump dramatically.

▶ **Billing Cycle**—This represents the length of time between each billing statement. A billing cycle is typically 30 days.

▶ **Credit Limit (or Credit Line)**—When you receive a new credit card, this is the maximum amount of credit the issuer is making available to you. The credit limit will depend on a number of factors, primarily your credit history (credit score). Periodically, the card issuer will increase or decrease your credit line based on your payment history.

▶ **Customer Service**—Many credit card companies offer 24-hour customer service that's available seven days per week via telephone or the Internet. Others offer limited hours when customer service is available. Ideally, you want to work with a card issuer that is available anytime to answer your questions and deal with issues that may arise.

▶ **Grace Period**—A *grace period* is the number of days the card issuer doesn't charge you interest on purchases. When applying for any credit card, be sure to read the fine print. Some credit card issuers give you a grace period only if your account is paid up and doesn't have a balance carried over from the previous month.

▶ **Introductory APR**—To encourage you to apply for its credit card (as opposed to the competition's), many credit card issuers offer special introductory deals for the first three months, six months, or one year you use their card. This is a temporary, usually low, interest rate (expressed as a yearly rate). Remember, the introductory rate you're offered will typically expire after a predetermined amount of time. After this introductory period, the APR you're responsible for will increase, sometimes significantly.

▶ **Late Fee**—If you're late on making your monthly payments, the card issuer has the right to impose various fees. In addition, if you're late on payments several times in a predefined period, your APR could automatically increase as well. In addition to charging late fees, the credit card issuer will report late payments to the credit bureaus, which will be reflected on your credit report.

▶ **Other Fees**—When reviewing any credit card application, read the fine print to determine if there are any other fees or hidden charges you'll be responsible for. An example of an additional fee is if you use the charge card to obtain a cash advance. There may also be a small monthly fee associated with the card, whether or not you use it.

▶ **Over Limit Fee**—If your credit limit is $1,500, for example, and your balance goes to $1,600 as a result of too many purchases or various fees being added to your balance, you will be charged an additional *over limit fee* by most credit card companies.

Chances are you receive a new credit card offer in the mail at least once or twice per week. In addition, you probably see ads on TV and all kinds of offers when surfing the Net. Make sure you apply for a credit card that offers you the best possible deal, based on your credit rating and needs. You can research various credit card offers by visiting these free Websites:

▶ Bank Rates—*www.bankrate.com.*

▶ Card Locator—*www.cardlocator.com.*

▶ Card Offers: The Credit Card Directory— *www.cardoffers.com.*

▶ Credit Cards Plus—*www.credit-cards-plus.com.*

▶ CreditLand—*www.credit-land.com.*

▶ The Credit Card Catalog—*www.creditcardcatalog.com.*

Protecting Your Credit

Your ability to obtain credit in the future will depend tremendously on how well you manage what credit you have right now. Whether or not you use your credit responsibly is entirely up to you. Abusing your credit cards now by making late payments or overspending will hurt your chances of obtaining a car loan, qualifying for a mortgage, or getting additional credit cards in the future.

To learn more about how to successfully manage your credit and repair your damaged credit, The Federal Citizen Information Center offers the following free brochures that you can download from the Internet (or call 1-888-878-3256 to order a printed version for a small fee):

▶ *Building a Better Credit Record— www.pueblo.gsa.gov/cic_text/money/credit-record/crrecord.htm.*

▶ *Credit Matters— www.pueblo.gsa.gov/cic_text/money/credit-report/rscredit.htm.*

▶ *How To Dispute Credit Report Errors— www.pueblo.gsa.gov/cic_text/money/credit-errors/crediter.htm.*

▶ *ID Theft: When Bad Things Happen to Your Good Name— www.pueblo.gsa.gov/cic_text/money/id-theft/idtheft.htm.*

▶ *Credit and Divorce— www.pueblo.gsa.gov/cic_text/money/divorce/divorce.htm.*

When It Rains, It Pours: Dealing With Unexpected Financial Hardships

No matter how successful you are, what type of job you have, where you live, how smart you are, how hard you work, or how dedicated you are to achieving success, there will be times in your life when the unexpected happens. Dealing with an emergency can be costly and extremely stressful. There are things you can do to help prevent emergencies or undesirable events from taking place, but it's important to always be financially prepared to deal with unexpected negative situations that are beyond your control.

This chapter focuses on preparing for and dealing with financial hardships and unexpected events before they happen. The objective is to help ensure your finances will be able to support you when and if something happens that has the potential to damage or destroy your financial well-being.

The topic of having insurance has been brought up already. The importance of having the necessary insurance in place cannot be stressed enough. Even if you're drastically trying to cut expenses and reduce your cost of living, you never want to eliminate insurance that protects your health, home, and property. Without health insurance, a trip to the hospital for a broken bone, for example, could cost you thousands of dollars.

If you're not properly insured, even a mild fender bender when driving your car could wind up costing thousands if you find yourself at fault and on the losing end of lawsuits.

The goal of this chapter isn't to scare you or transform you into a fanatic who is convinced the worst is about to happen. Instead, the purpose of this chapter is to help you develop a strategy to protect your financial security when and if something negative does happen. When confronted with an unexpected financial emergency, make sure your most important financial needs are met first. In other words, worry first about your mortgage or rent, food, medical expenses (if applicable), insurance premiums, and your utility bills.

Planning for Emergencies

There are many types of emergencies that could potentially impact your financial well-being. Sometimes events are as simple and as common as your child catching the flu, causing you to have to stay home from work to care for her. This could create a financial burden if you're forced to forfeit that day's paycheck. The best way to deal with these smaller emergencies is to spend time, in advance, thinking about what could happen and develop a plan for coping so that the financial impact is minimal.

For example, have a plan in place in case your child becomes ill and needs to stay home from school. Is there a relative or friend, for example, who could be on call to stay with your child so that you can still go to work? What happens if your car breaks down? Do you have someone you can call, last minute, to give you a ride to and from your job? These are common events that can be predicted and planned for so that the financial implications won't be severe.

Unfortunately, some events have the potential of being financially and emotionally devastating if not handled correctly. One of the best things you can do, starting immediately, to prepare yourself for virtually any type of financial emergency, is to establish a savings account or fund containing between three and six months worth of living expenses. This money should be readily accessible, should you need it. This is money that could be used for unexpected medical bills, car repairs, or to cover your living expenses if (for whatever reason) you can't work. These days, for people who get laid off or downsized, it's taking longer and longer to find a new job. Ideally, you want the funds in place to support yourself during your job search efforts.

Having the appropriate insurance policies to protect yourself, your home, your belongings, your vehicle, and, of course, your family against tragedy is also extremely important. Some of the types of insurance that are a necessity for most people include:

▸ Homeowner's Insurance (Renter's Insurance).

▸ Health Insurance (This could include a separate dental insurance policy).

▸ Automobile Insurance.

▸ Long-Term Disability Insurance.

▸ Life Insurance.

▸ An "Umbrella Policy"—This type of policy kicks in after your homeowner's and/or auto insurance and offers you additional coverage, typically up to $1 million or $2 million.

Because everyone's needs are different, to determine your own insurance needs, consult with several insurance brokers/advisors. Shop around for the best deals, but also ask about package deals where you obtain multiple types of policies from the same broker or insurance provider.

While you're financially stable and your credit is strong, if you already own a home, apartment, or condo, one way to make sure money will be available when you need it (in case of an emergency) is to establish an *equity line of credit* based on the equity you currently have in your home (or other property you own).

According to The Federal Reserve Board as stated on their Website (*www.federalreserve.gov/pubs/homeline*):

> "A home equity line of credit is a form of revolving credit in which your home serves as collateral. Because the home is likely to be a consumer's largest asset, many homeowners use their credit lines only for major items, such as education, home improvements, or medical bills and not for day-to-day expenses. With a home equity line, you will be approved for a specific amount of credit—your credit limit, the maximum amount you may borrow at any one time under the plan. Many lenders set the credit limit on a home equity line by taking a percentage (say, 75 percent) of the

home's appraised value and subtracting from that the balance owed on the existing mortgage. In determining your actual credit limit, the lender will also consider your ability to repay, by looking at your income, debts, and other financial obligations as well as your credit history.

"Many home equity plans set a fixed period during which you can borrow money, such as 10 years. At the end of this 'draw period,' you may be allowed to renew the credit line. If your plan does not allow renewals, you will not be able to borrow additional money once the period has ended. Some plans may call for payment in full of any outstanding balance at the end of the period. Others may allow repayment over a fixed period (the "repayment period"), for example, 10 years. Once approved for a home equity line of credit, you will most likely be able to borrow up to your credit limit whenever you want. Typically, you will use special checks to draw on your line. Under some plans, borrowers can use a credit card or other means to draw on the line.

"There may be limitations on how you use the line. Some plans may require you to borrow a minimum amount each time you draw on the line (for example, $300) and to keep a minimum amount outstanding. Some plans may also require that you take an initial advance when the line is set up."

If you're able to secure an equity line of credit, don't consider this free money! Instead, have the credit line in place, but only use it in an emergency, when funds are seriously needed. There is no charge to have an equity line of credit in place. You only pay fees and interest once you start borrowing this money and using it. Because the process for obtaining an equity line of credit is very similar to obtaining any type of loan, those with the best credit rating and the most equity in their home will be privy to the best deals from the various financial institutions that offer this type of loan. Just like any type of credit, a home equity loan has an APR as well as other fees associated with it.

Utilizing a home equity loan (or even your credit cards, in cases when money is needed for an emergency) is a lot more economically feasible than tapping into your retirement account(s) for the emergency money. Borrowing money or withdrawing money from your IRA early, for example, can involve having to pay high fees, taxes, and penalties. This should be a last resort. Consult a financial specialist before doing this so you understand the financial implications.

Emergencies Worth Planning For

While any or all of these emergencies could potentially happen to you and your family, hopefully they never will. It's important, however, to have a financial plan in place for when the worst does happen. Some of the larger-scale tragedies you should be financially prepared to deal with are discussed in the following sections.

Serious Illness or Injury

What would happen to your financial stability if you were forced to be on an unpaid leave of absence from work for two weeks, two months, or even a year or more? There are several things you can do to help protect yourself financially, should you experience a serious illness or injury.

First, evaluate the coverage offered through whatever health insurance you currently have, and make sure it's adequate. You might want to sit down with one or two insurance brokers or specialists and carefully evaluate your needs. Also, determine if you're entitled to any state or federally subsidized benefits relating to medical coverage.

In addition to health insurance, many employers offer worker's compensation and/or long-term disability insurance. Determine right now if this is a benefit you're entitled to should something happen. Assuming you qualify for this type of benefit, determine how much coverage you'd receive. Would this coverage be adequate to protect you and your family financially for several months or even years? If not, you might consider purchasing additional long-term disability insurance. It's true, this additional insurance would be an out-of-pocket expense on an ongoing basis, but you'll be protecting yourself (and your family) in case something happens that would keep you from working and earning your regular paycheck.

According to the 4 Disability Insurance Quotes Website (*www.4-disability-insurance-quotes.com* or phone 1-800-544-1662):

> "Disability Income Insurance is insurance coverage that
> provides monthly payments, up to a specified amount, and
> for a specific time period after a covered illness or injury

occurs. Insurance must be purchased *prior* to your illness or injury. Disability Insurance provides a way to protect your income and your standard of living. Disability Insurance protects your most valuable asset—you, and your ability to earn income. If you become disabled, you most likely will not be able to earn enough income to cover your continued living expenses. Disability Income Insurance will provide monthly payments to help meet your daily living expenses."

Unemployment or Salary Reduction

Based on recent domestic and world events and the condition of the economy, companies of all sizes continue to downsize, reorganize, or shut down, leaving countless workers suddenly unemployed. In some situations, people are able to keep their jobs, but are forced to accept a significant salary reduction. Either one of these scenarios can have serious financial implications on you and your family.

Pay attention to your employment situation. Are major changes happening within your company that could put your job in jeopardy? Have you heard rumors that a reorganization plan may take place or that the company plans to downsize or merge in the not-so-distant future? As soon as it becomes clear that you may not have the job security you want and need, consider taking a proactive approach by starting to look for alternate job opportunities. Don't wait until the worst happens. It's always easier to find a new job and research possible opportunities if you're currently employed and have a regular paycheck coming in.

Of course, knowing you have enough money in savings to support yourself for one, two, or three months while you're looking for a new job and have no paycheck coming will also give you some added peace of mind. If you don't have any savings in place, start creating an alternative financial plan in case you suddenly become unemployed. Take into account unemployment benefits and/or the severance package you're entitled to, then focus on alternate income options (such as working a temp job through a temporary employment agency).

In situations where you're forced to take a salary reduction, immediately focus on lowering your living expenses by reevaluating your budget and making cuts wherever possible. Focus on the strategies discussed in Chapters 2 and 3, as well as those that will be discussed in Chapter 5. Ideally, you need to be able to support yourself with your now lower paycheck, without relying on your credit cards (and building up debt) or tapping too heavily into your savings. This might mean making some drastic budgetary changes, such as trading in your vehicle for a less expensive model (with lower monthly payments) and cutting out all frivolous and noncritical spending.

As soon as it becomes evident that your job may not be secure, start developing plans based on possible scenarios such as losing your job due to downsizing. What unemployment benefits or severance pay, if any, are you entitled to? When would you begin receiving these benefits? From a financial standpoint, determine which of your bills absolutely must continue to be paid, no matter what, and focus on reducing your spending. It might also be a good idea to restructure your outstanding debt to lower or temporarily defer payments.

While you're dealing with the financial burdens of unemployment or receiving a lower salary, also pay attention to the future. Immediately start updating your resume and focusing on methods of landing a new job or supplementing your salary. For example, consider working with a temporary employment agency or taking on a second job in order to bring in the money you need to cover your living expenses, even after you've reworked your budget. Working a temp job is a fast and easy way to earn money while also looking for a steady full-time position. A large percentage of people who prove themselves while working a temp job ultimately get offered a full-time position with that employer.

Immediately take steps to find the best possible new job. Take a multi-faceted approach to your job search effort by responding to "help wanted" ads, utilizing career-related Websites, attending job fairs, contacting head-hunters, working with employment agencies, and, most importantly, net-working (contacting friends and relatives, along with former coworkers, educators, clients, customers, and so on). Many of the career-related Websites, such as The Monster Board (*www.monster.com*), offer an abundance of information and advice to job seekers. It's important to remember that if you lose your job as a result of downsizing or your employer going out of business, future employers will not hold that against you during your job search, so be open and honest about your predicament. Also, be sure to take full advantage of whatever job placement services or career counseling that is offered by the employer that laid you off. Career counseling is often also available to alumni of high schools and colleges.

Divorce/Separation

A divorce or legal separation can have a major impact on your financial stability, because a couple that was once living together (utilizing one or two incomes) now must support two separate households. In addition, there are a wide range of tax implications involved with a divorce or separation, so be sure to consult with your attorney as well as a financial advisor. Issues that need to be addressed involve the division of assets and who will take responsibility for your family's debts.

One of the only ways you can "prepare" for the financial implications of a divorce is for both parties to sign a prenuptial agreement prior to getting married. This puts a financial plan in place should something go wrong with the marriage. Even with such an agreement, it is important for both parties to work together (in conjunction with their lawyers, accountants, and financial advisors) to ensure everyone's financial protection and well-being after the divorce or separation.

Death of a Spouse

The death of a loved one will have a tremendous emotional impact that will last for months or perhaps years. However, if you are financially prepared, hopefully this unexpected loss will not result in financial devastation. Part of every family's budget should include ample life insurance policies that will financially protect the surviving member(s) of the family.

Too many families experience sudden financial hardship because they thought that a tragedy could never happen to their family. Life insurance is relatively inexpensive and is something that you should have. An insurance specialist or financial consultant will be able to assist you in determining your coverage needs and the best type of life insurance to obtain. The Insure.com Website (*www.insure.com/life/lifeneedsestimator/*) offers a free "Life Insurance Needs Estimator Tool" that can help you select the appropriate coverage you and your family's needs.

According to the Insure.com Website:

> "The main reason for owning life insurance is to provide income replacement to your beneficiaries when you die. But if you are interested in estate planning, cash accumulation, wealth transfer, and estate tax liquidity, life insurance can also help you achieve these goals. Life insurance policies are now available from more than 2,000 life insurance

companies in the United States, as well as from financial institutions, like banks. It's just as important to understand the companies behind the products as it is to understand the products themselves."

In addition to insurance, adults should have a will in place, plus consider various options relating to estate planning.

Natural Disasters/Terrorism

The tragedies of September 11th have changed the way most Americans think in terms of their safety and well-being as they go about their everyday lives. Like so many people living elsewhere in the world, Americans now live with the ongoing threat of terrorism. To prepare yourself, there are a wide range of things you can do, such as having adequate supplies in your home. The Red Cross offers the Prepare.org Website (*www.prepare.org*) to help you prepare for unexpected natural disasters or terrorism. The United States Government's Department of Homeland Security also supports an informative Website, called Ready.gov (*www.ready.gov*) to help individuals and families prepare for any type of disaster, especially related to terrorism.

In terms of your finances, it's an excellent idea to keep some cash hidden somewhere in your home that can be used for emergencies. It's also important to keep copies of all of your important financial documents (including bank statements and insurance records, for example) in one place, in an organized manner. You might consider investing in a small, fire- and water-proof safe in which to store these items. You can purchase a small safe from any office superstore for between $50 and $100 dollars.

The Implications of Financial Hardship

Developing and living with financial hardships is stressful, especially if you're not able to pay your bills on time. You become too reliant on your savings or credit to cover your day-to-day expenses, or you don't have a plan for getting yourself out of your predicament. Once you start getting too behind on your bills, collections people start calling your home incessantly, from 8 a.m. to 9 p.m., often seven days a week. You'll also start getting bombarded with collection letters in the mail, not to mention your regular bills. Furthermore, the later you get on your payments, the worse situation you create for yourself in terms of your credit rating.

According to The Federal Trade Commission's Website (*www.ftc.gov*):

"A collector may contact you in person, by mail, telephone, telegram, or fax. However, a debt collector may not contact you at inconvenient times or places, such as before 8 a.m. or after 9 p.m., unless you agree. A debt collector also may not contact you at work if the collector knows that your employer disapproves. You can stop a debt collector from contacting you by writing a letter to the collection agency telling them to stop. Once the agency receives your letter, they may not contact you again except to say there will be no further contact or to notify you that the debt collector or creditor intends to take some specific action. Please note, however, that sending such a letter to a collector does not make the debt go away if you actually owe it. You could still be sued by the debt collector or your original creditor."

If you get too deep in debt and become unable to pay your bills, chances are, you not only will begin stressing about the reason(s) why you got into the financial crisis, such as losing your job, but the stress involved with managing your finances will also intensify. To protect yourself, develop a game plan for handling the situation, address one problem at a time, and focus on working toward a solution.

It's all too common for people to simply ignore their financial problems. This is probably the worst thing you could do. Instead, reevaluate your budget, determine how and where your income will be coming from in the immediate future, and then make contact with the organizations you owe money to in order to make special arrangements. When contacting your creditors, be prepared to negotiate in good faith so you can eventually cover your debt and protect your credit rating.

For example, if you lose your job and have no immediate source of income, some credit card companies will be extremely lenient, allowing you to temporarily pay extra-low minimum payments on what you owe. These companies might also offer you an extra low interest rate and/or waive late fees (or other fees) to keep your debt from getting out of control. If you demonstrate a willingness to make good on your debts and make a point to negotiate, the harassment you'd otherwise receive from your creditors will be kept to a minimum. Try to create a win-win situation with your creditors, one at a time, and confirm whatever agreement you come to in writing. Keep in mind, you may be able to negotiate a debt settlement with your credit card companies. This means you pay only a percentage of what you actually owe to the creditor. While this can quickly help your financial situation, it will negatively impact your credit rating for several years to come and will typically result in the loss of credit by that creditor.

In terms of your utilities (gas, electric, and telephone), contact these providers and discuss your financial situation. You may be entitled to special discounts as a result of your financial hardship, especially if it relates to illness. Also, determine if any local, state, or federal assistance is available to you in terms of subsidies, and so on.

During times of financial crisis, try to keep a positive attitude. If necessary, talk to someone about the stresses you're experiencing and try to work with a legitimate financial advisor or credit counselor who can help you get through the financial aspect of your crisis as quickly and as easily as possible, without making matters worse. Beware of those ads for credit counseling firms that guarantee unrealistic results. Make sure you're working with a reputable financial or credit counselor or advisor. Appendix A of this book offers advice for hiring someone to advise you on your finances, such as an accountant or Certified Financial Planner.

Your Next Steps

If you're in the midst of dealing with any type of financial problem, that should be your priority. However, at your earliest convenience, it's important to start developing plans in case the unexpected happens. Based on your own situation, create a to-do checklist for yourself relating to what financial planning and actions need to be taken, as soon as possible, to prepare for unexpected tragedies. After your list is created, prioritize that list and start putting your strategies into effect to ensure your financial protection. For example, one item on your list might be to contact an insurance specialist about obtaining life insurance policies for yourself and your spouse. Another item might involve establishing an emergency cash fund and contributing a small amount to that fund with every future paycheck.

Preparing for Financial Hardships To-Do List

Use the following worksheet to compile a to-do checklist of financial plans that need to be made.

What needs to be done:

_____

_____

_____

_____

Step(s) that need to be taken:

_____

_____

_____

_____

_____

Deadline for developing and implementing your plan:

_____

Results:

_____

_____

_____

_____

What needs to be done:

_____

_____

_____

_____

Step(s) that need to be taken:

_____

_____

_____

_____

_____

_____

Deadline for developing and implementing your plan:

_____

Results:

_____

_____

_____

_____

What needs to be done:

_____

_____

_____

_____

_____

Step(s) that need to be taken:

_____

_____

_____

_____

_____

_____

Deadline for developing and implementing your plan:

_____

Results:

_____

_____

_____

_____

What needs to be done:

_____

_____

_____

_____

_____

Step(s) that need to be taken:

_____

_____

_____

_____

_____

_____

Deadline for developing and implementing your plan:

_____

Results:

_____

_____

_____

_____

What needs to be done:

_____

_____

_____

_____

_____

Step(s) that need to be taken:

_____

_____

_____

_____

_____

_____

Deadline for developing and implementing your plan:

_____

Results:

_____

_____

_____

_____

5

Becoming Thrifty Doesn't Make You a Cheapskate

Taking the money you currently earn and being able to make the most of it is one of the best reasons to develop and maintain a budget. By cutting your expenses, you'll have more discretionary income, which can then be used in a variety of ways to improve your overall financial situation. This chapter is all about taking the everyday expenses you already have and finding ways to reduce them. You'll find the information offered here can be used in conjunction with what you learned in Chapter 2. Remember, by cutting expenses, you should be able to increase your discretionary income. How you utilize your discretionary income will play a determining role in your future financial prosperity.

Finding ways to cut your expenses will take a bit of creativity on your part, especially if you want to save money but not negatively impact your current standard of living. In general, always be on the lookout for bargains, take advantage of sales and special promotions, and know your needs and how to satisfy them without overindulging.

Saving Money in Everyday Life

No matter what you need to buy, if you invest time and energy into shopping around for the best possible deals, you will almost always save money.

When making large purchases (for such things as major appliances), do research about what you're buying and look for quality, durability, warranty, energy efficiency, and reliability. Learn as much as you can about what you're buying by reading a magazine such as *Consumer Reports* (*www.consumerreports.org*). To save money over the long term, in some cases it will make economic sense to spend a bit more up front when making a purchase, if you know you'll save money in the months and years to come. For example, you might spend several dollars more up front for an energy efficient lightbulb, but that single bulb will last five times longer than a cheaper, less efficient bulb, plus save electricity and cut your energy bill. Thus, the long-term savings on that single lightbulb are far greater than the initial investment you made.

As you make your purchases, think about how they're being paid for. If you're using a credit card or financing your purchase, will you be paying off the balance immediately or will you be paying interest charges over a period of time? If you're financing your purchase, also calculate the amount of interest and additional fees you'll be paying and add them to the actual price of what you're buying.

When making a purchase, ask yourself these questions:

▸ Is the purchase absolutely necessary?

▸ Do you have the money to afford what you're buying?

▸ What options are available to save money when making this purchase? Can you use coupons or take advantage of a sale or special promotion?

▸ Is there a similar product or service that would be less expensive?

▸ Have you done the necessary research to ensure that you're getting exactly what you need at the best possible price?

▸ What benefit(s) will you receive from the purchase?

▸ What category does this expense fall into—Absolutely Necessary, Important, Not Critical, or Frivolous?

The LowerMyBills.com (*www.lowermybills.com*) and BillSaver.com (*www.billsaver.com*) Websites are two clearinghouses for quickly finding the best deals on a wide range of products and services including long-distance telephone service, home refinancing, various types of insurance, credit cards, Internet services, and debt consolidation services. In addition to using these sites, following are some strategies for saving money in regard to various popular expense categories.

Automobile Expenses

▸ Compare prices at local gas stations. Use the lowest octane gas recommended for your vehicle—in most cases, Regular Unleaded. On certain days, some gas stations offer a discount per gallon of gas. Additional discounts or rebates are applied if you pay for your gas using that gas station's own charge card. For example, if you use a Shell MasterCard at Shell gas stations, you'll receive at least a five-percent rebate on your gas purchases. As long as you pay that credit card bill promptly and incur no interest charges, using a gas charge card will save you money.

▸ Become a member of a roadside assistance plan, such as AAA (*www.aaa.com* or 1-800-222-8252). If you get stuck and need to be towed, get a flat tire, or run out of gas, you'll save a fortune getting the roadside services you need.

▸ Keep your car tuned up and change the oil regularly. Also, keep the tire pressure at the recommended levels. This will help enhance your vehicle's fuel efficiency and save you at least $100 per year in gas.

▸ If you've financed the purchase of your vehicle and if interest rates go down (or your credit rating improves) during the period of the loan, consider refinancing your vehicle to lower your monthly payments and the overall amount you'll ultimately be spending on your car.

Banking

▸ Many banks will reduce or eliminate monthly fees for a checking account if you maintain a predefined minimum balance between all of your accounts (checking, savings, and so on) with that bank. This can save you up to $25 per month. If you arrange to have your paycheck directly deposited into your checking account, some banks will wave or reduce the monthly fees for that account.

▶ Ask to see a list of all fees from your bank for each of your accounts. This includes fees for using a teller, ATM machine, having a checking account, online banking, telephone banking, and so forth. Don't just assume that because you have an account with a bank it will offer you the lowest fees and interest rates on a credit card or some other type of loan. Be sure to shop around for the best rates for all of your banking and investment needs.

▶ To find credit cards offered by banks and other financial institutions that have the most desirable fees and interest rates, point your Web browser to *www.cardlocator.com or www.bankrate.com*.

Clothes Shopping

When it comes to shopping for clothes, there are many ways of saving money by becoming a savvy shopper. First and foremost, wait for sales! Around every major holiday and in between seasons, for example, all of the department stores and popular chain stores at the mall offer sales. Take advantage of them! In addition, be sure to utilize coupons offered by major retailers.

Other money-saving strategies for clothes shopping include:

▶ Avoid designer labels. Often, you can find the same styles and fashions (without the designer label) for much less money.

▶ Shop at outlet stores. Across America, outlet malls are opening. These outlets typically offer substantial savings on designer labels and name-brand fashions.

▶ Don't buy entirely new outfits when you can buy accessories or mix and match garments to create additional outfits using garments already in your wardrobe.

▶ Buy quality and evergreen clothing items that will last and that won't go out of style in two or three months. You can dress fashionably without being too trendy or following every single fad.

▶ Shop at discount stores. Places like T.J. Maxx, Ross, Syms, Men's Warehouse, Burlington Coat Factory, and Marshalls offer the same designer fashions as major department stores, but often at drastically reduced prices.

▶ Set a clothing budget for yourself and stick to it. Many people buy clothing spontaneously. Instead, when you go shopping for clothes, know exactly what types of outfits or garments you need and then shop around for the best deals.

▶ Plan ahead. If you know you will need a heavy coat for next winter, for example, the best time to purchase this is during the off-season.

Grocery Shopping

As a general rule, those convenience stores that are open late at night tend to charge the most money for staple food items such as milk. To save money, shop at the least expensive grocery store in your area and be sure to take advantage of coupons and the frequent shopper cards offered by supermarkets.

Other money-saving tips for grocery shopping include:

▶ Compare labels and price tags. Shop based on price per ounce or unit cost. This information is displayed on the shelf labels. It's typically cheaper to buy a larger container of an item.

▶ Prepare a shopping list, in advance, and stick to it. Avoid spontaneous purchases.

▶ Take advantage of sales and coupons, but only buy items you need and use. If there's a two-for-the-price-of-one sale on an item, it may be a good deal, but if you don't typically use the product, don't buy it.

▶ Consider purchasing generic brands or supermarket brands for certain products. The ingredients/quality of these products are often identical to the name-brand products, but you can save a lot of money.

▶ On items you use a lot, consider buying in bulk to save money. For some nonperishable items, you might want to shop at Costco or B.J.'s Wholesale Club, for example, to buy in bulk if your supermarket doesn't sell the staple items you use frequently in bulk.

▶ Take advantage of online grocery coupons as well as the ones that appear in circulars and newspapers. To find coupons online, visit these Websites:

- ▸ *www.valupage.com.*

- ▸ *www.coupons.com.*

- ▸ *www.centsoff.com.*

- ▸ *www.coolsavings.com.*

Holiday Spending

It's easy to get caught up in the holiday season and spend too much on gifts and celebrations. Based on your available budget, see page 97 for a worksheet that will help you preplan your holiday spending. Use this worksheet in advance to develop your holiday spending budget and then to track actual holiday spending throughout each holiday season.

Insurance

As you look over your monthly expenses (compiled in Chapters 1 and 2), you've probably noticed you're spending a good portion of your income on various types of insurance. In today's society, insurance is critical to your long-term financial well-being, because it's the insurance you have that financially protects you when things go wrong.

Some of the popular types of insurance most people have include:

▶ Homeowner's/Renter's Insurance.

▶ Health Insurance.

▶ Auto Insurance.

▶ Life Insurance.

▶ Dental Insurance.

▶ Long-Term Disability Insurance.

The first step to saving money on your insurance premiums (what you pay for each policy) is to obtain only the coverage you need. This can be done by sitting down with multiple insurance brokers and having them conduct a free evaluation of those needs. Between your various policies, make sure all of your assets are amply covered, including yourself, as well as your

Holiday Budget Worksheet

Category	Available Budget ($)	Amount Actually Spent ($)
Gifts for Family		
Gifts for Friends		
Gifts for Coworkers/ Superiors		
Gift Wrapping Supplies		
Shipping Costs (for gifts)		
Holiday Meal(s)		
Christmas Tree		
Outdoor Decorations & Lights		
Indoor Decorations & Lights (including tree trimmings)		
Party Clothes		
Holiday Activities		
Holiday Travel		
Holiday-Related Entertainment		
TOTALS:		

family, home, belongings, valuables, vehicle, and other assets. You'll then want to shop around for the best possible coverage offered at the lowest premiums.

One way to quickly cut your insurance premiums is to acquire policies with higher deductibles. This is the amount of a claim you need to pay (out of pocket) before your insurance kicks in. If you have a $1,000 deductible on your auto insurance policy, for example, if you need to file a claim as a result of an accident, the first $1,000 comes directly out of your pocket. Choosing your deductible for each type of insurance policy is a personal decision, based on your willingness to deal with risk and ability to cover your expenses should something go wrong. The lower your deductibles, the higher your regular insurance premiums will be.

Aside from shopping around for the best rates and policies once you clearly define your needs, ask about discounts offered if you use the same broker (or insurance company) for multiple types of policies. As you shop for an insurance policy of any type, make sure you ask plenty of questions. Understand exactly what will be covered and what isn't covered. It's important to know what the policy's limits are (in terms of the maximum amount of money the insurance company will be responsible for), what the process is for filing a claim, and how reputable the insurance company is. Finally, ask the insurance broker about ways to further reduce your premiums once you've selected your policies. For homeowner's insurance, you'll save money, for example, if you install a burglar alarm.

Low-Cost Telephone Service

Both local and long-distance telephone services have been deregulated. Now, you can shop around for the best deals on your home telephone service, based on your needs. Be sure to ask about packages that combine popular services such as caller ID and call-waiting, with low monthly fees and competitive rates for local, in-state, and long-distance calls.

Before shopping for the best deals, determine what your calling habits are. Be sure to differentiate between local, in-state, long-distance, calling card calls, and international calls. Determine where you call the most and what times of the day or night you make the majority of your calls. Review your past phone bills for this information.

If you make a lot of local (or in-state calls), look into an unlimited local calling plan. Your local phone service may come from a different company than the one that provides your long-distance service. Depending on the long-distance service you subscribe to, you could pay anywhere from $.03 to $.25 (or more) per minute. Be sure to ask about billing increments and look for a long-distance service that bills in 6-second or 10-second increments, as opposed to by-the-minute.

While most people are familiar with long distance from AT&T, Sprint, and MCI (which, at the time this book was written, was still offering long-distance services), you can often obtain better long-distance rates from lesser known companies, like IDT (1-888-640-6929 or *www.idt.net*), Capsule Communications (1-877-937-7707) or LongDistance.com (1-800-466-1550 or *www.longdistance.com*).

Look for a long-distance service with very low (or zero) monthly fees and the lowest per-minute charges with the smallest billing increments. To shop around for the best deals available, point your Web browser to *www.lowermybills.com* to see a price comparison for dozens of long-distance phone companies.

Finally, when shopping for a phone service, ask about package deals and promotional deals. For example, MCI offers the Neighborhood service (1-877-777-6271 or *www.theneighborhood.com*), which, for a flat monthly fee, includes unlimited local, in-state, and long-distance calls. Other companies will offer money-saving bundles or a predetermined number of long-distance minutes for a flat fee. To obtain the very lowest long-distance rates (less than $.05 per minute), you may be required to have your monthly bill automatically billed to your major credit card or arrange to have the funds automatically withdrawn from your checking account.

Depending on your phone usage, by shopping around for the best deals on local, in-state, long-distance, calling-card, and international calls, you can often save hundreds of dollars per year. Keep in mind that, if your phone usage tends to be high, it might make sense to have different companies provide different services. Your calling card may come from one company, while your local and long-distance service is provided by other companies. Before signing up for a service, be sure to read all of the fine print, to ensure there are no hidden charges or additional service fees, then carefully review your phone bill(s).

Just about everyone these days has a cell phone. Most people with average or above-average credit can obtain regular wireless phone service from a company such as Sprint PCS, Cingular, T-Mobile, Nextel, AT&T Wireless, or Verizon Wireless. Because the industry has become so competitive, there are always great deals to be had, especially if you're willing to sign a one- or two-year service agreement with a single service provider. Things to look for when shopping around for the best wireless phone deal include:

▶ The coverage area of the network, especially if you'll be traveling with your phone to other areas within your state or to other states.

▶ The number of daytime or "anytime" minutes offered with the plan. These are minutes used for making calls on weekdays, during daytime hours.

▶ The number of night and weekend minutes offered with the plan. Ideally, you want unlimited service on nights and weekends, plus holidays.

▶ Whether or not long-distance calls are included in the plan. Ideally, you should pay no additional long-distance fees.

▶ Whether or not there are roaming charges associated with the plan if you leave a specific calling area.

▶ The length of the service contract you need to sign. Because rates are always dropping and new services are constantly being introduced, avoid signing an agreement for a term longer than one year. If you break your service contract, there is often a one-time fee of at least $150.

▶ Evaluate any special promotions, such as "roll-over minutes," unlimited free PCS-to-PCS calls, shared minutes between family members, and so on, that are offered with the various plans. Make sure you're paying only for services and features you want or need.

▶ As long as you stay with the same service provider, make sure you can change calling plans without financial penalties.

▶ How much it costs per-minute if you exceed the number of minutes offered in your plan. Abusing your wireless phone is the biggest reason why people wind up with huge monthly bills, so be careful! Once you use up your monthly allocated minutes, you could be billed up to $.65 per minute (or more), plus long-distance charges, for each additional minute you use.

Once you choose your wireless phone service plan, always be on the lookout for better (more competitive) plans with that same provider. Limited time promotions are always being offered. Also, keep in mind that prepaid wireless phone service is always more expensive than signing up for a regular plan. One of the best ways to save money on your wireless phone bill is to use the phone as little as possible during the weekday daytime period, but take advantage of unlimited nights and weekend usage. For about $30 per month, you'll be able to easily find a plan with about 300 daytime (or anytime) minutes, plus unlimited nights and weekends, with long distance included.

Finally, consider purchasing the optional insurance for your telephone handset to protect it against damage or theft. This will increase your monthly charges by no more than $4, but you'll save up to several hundred dollars if and when you need to repair or replace your actual phone.

Refinancing Your Home

If you have a mortgage, you might be able to save hundreds of dollars every month (thousands over the life of the loan) simply by refinancing at a lower APR or changing the length of your mortgage. For many people, refinancing a mortgage every few years makes economic sense, but it depends on what your long-term financial goals are and where mortgage rates are at. Your credit rating will play a large role in your ability to obtain a mortgage or refinance at the best possible rates. To learn where mortgage rates are right now, visit the "Mortgage Refi" area of the BankRate.com Website at *www.bankrate.com*. This site also offers a free mortgage calculator which will help you calculate your monthly payments based upon the total mortgage amount, loan type, term, and interest rate.

You should consider refinancing if you can get a rate that is at least 1.5 percentage points lower than your existing mortgage or if you want to switch from a 30-year to a 20-year or 15-year loan in order to build equity faster and pay off the loan in a shorter period of time.

Before refinancing, it's important to do the necessary calculations to ensure that you'll save money once you include the additional fees and expenses involved, such as points, application/processing fees, and closing costs. Don't get caught up in the hype from various mortgage brokers. Shop around for the best deals, ask questions, and make sure you're getting exactly what was promised before signing the papers. It's an excellent idea to have an accountant or real estate attorney review the paperwork before refinancing.

Some of the reasons people consider refinancing include:

▶ Wanting to take advantage of lower rates that weren't available when you first obtained the mortgage. This will allow you to lower your monthly payments.

▶ You'd like to switch from an *adjustable-rate mortgage* (ARM) to a *fixed-rate loan*. With a fixed-rate loan, you'll know exactly what your payment will be for the entire life of the loan—it won't change. Fixed rate loans are usually offered for 15-, 20-, and 30-year periods. An adjustable-rate loan (also known as a *variable-rate loan*), typically offers a lower initial interest rate than fixed-rate loans. The interest rate, however, will fluctuate (sometimes dramatically) over the life of the loan, based on market conditions. When interest rates rise, so will your monthly loan payments. Likewise, when interest rates fall, your monthly payments will decrease.

▶ You hope to build up equity in your home faster by converting to a loan with a shorter term and/or lower rate.

▶ Take advantage of the equity you've built up in your house to get cash. While the amount of your mortgage will increase, you can use the funds to pay off much higher interest loans (such as credit card debt), or pay for a big-ticket item such as a wedding, home improvement, or your child's education. If done correctly, you can save money. In this situation, also consider a home equity loan, home equity line of credit, or a second mortgage. Determine which type of loan offers you the best rates and options, based on your credit rating and needs.

Be sure to shop around for the best refinancing deals. This is an extremely competitive industry. Once you know the type of mortgage and the rates you're looking for and qualify for (based on your credit score and payment history), contact multiple lenders and mortgage brokers. As you'll discover, there are typically a handful of fees involved with refinancing. Sometimes these fees will be out-of-pocket expenses for you. In many situations, however, the fees can be built into the new loan. Points (fees paid to the lender), closing costs, attorney's fees, land survey/appraisal fees, loan origination fees, and Private Mortgage Insurance (PMI) are among the costs you need to take into consideration.

To learn more about refinancing, a free booklet can be downloaded from The Federal Reserve Board by pointing your Web browser to *www.pueblo.gsa.gov/cic_text/housing/best-mortgage/mortb_1.htm*.

From the BankRate.com Website, additional information about whether or not you can financially benefit from refinancing your mortgage can be found at *www.bankrate.com/brm/news/checkup/mortgage5.asp*.

Travel

As a result of the airlines doing poorly, the growing popularity of Internet-based travel sites, and a wide range of other factors, air travel has never been cheaper. Using the Internet to plan your next getaway, you can easily save more than 60 percent, as opposed to using a travel agent or calling an airline, hotel, and/or car-rental company directly. You can even save a fortune on all-inclusive resort vacations, cruises, and international travel. In fact, you may find it cheaper to fly from New York to London than it is to fly from New York to Orlando, for example, depending on the various promotions happening within the travel industry. Also, using these online services, you can often book a four-star hotel for the price of a two- or three-star hotel.

Once you decide on your overall travel budget and have a general idea of your destination, start shopping around and be persistent. When booking travel, here are some basic money-saving strategies:

▶ Call the airline, hotel, rental car company, cruise line, or resort directly and get their best price over the telephone. If you're a frequent flier, for example, ask about special promotions or offers.

▶ Visit that companies' Website and look for online-only travel deals and specials.

▶ Contact a travel agent and ask for their recommendations and best deals.

▶ Visit the popular online travel sites. This is typically where you'll find the best deals. Keep in mind, when booking travel online, the traditional rules of getting the best deals by booking seven or 14 days in advance don't typically apply, and there's often no need for a Saturday night stay at your destination. You'll find that prices vary greatly between these sites and change from hour to hour, so shop around. One drawback to purchasing highly discounted airfares or hotels is that once they're booked and paid for, there are absolutely no changes, cancellations, or refunds allowed. Some of the popular travel-oriented Websites that offer great deals on airfares, hotels, rental cars, cruises, and all-inclusive resort vacations include: Expedia (*www.expedia.com*), Hotwire (*www.hotwire.com*), Last Minute Travel (*www.lastminutetravel.com*), Orbitz (*www.orbitz.com*), Priceline (*www.priceline.com*), SideStep (*www.sidestep.com*), and Travelocity (*www.travelocity.com*).

Long-Term Financial Planning

Developing a budget that allows you to cover your day-to-day living expenses is obviously a good idea. However, you also need to plan for the long term—the future. After all, in the years to come, chances are you'll need relatively large amounts of money for:

▶ Buying a car.

▶ Buying a home.

▶ Home improvements.

▶ Optional medical procedures (such as plastic surgery or cosmetic dental work).

▶ Paying for your child's education.

▶ Retirement.

▶ Vacations.

▶ Wedding.

Your ability to pay for these expenses will, in large part, be possible if you begin to allocate the necessary funds from your discretionary income, beginning immediately, and start saving. Think about what the future may have in store for you, and consider what large expenses you'll have down the road. Next, develop a financial plan so you'll be able to handle those expenses.

A financial advisor will be able to help you develop a long-term savings plan that might involve creating an investment strategy, depending on what your goals and time frame are. Some of your investment options include traditional bank savings accounts, CDs, mutual funds, stocks, and bonds. Each of these investment options potentially allow your money to grow, but involves a different level of risk. A savings account at your local bank, for example, is insured by the FDIC and has no risk associated with it. Unfortunately, this type of account typically pays very low interest. If you have money to put into savings for a long period (five years or more), you might consider an investment strategy that involves some greater risk in order to earn more money.

How you invest your discretionary income should depend upon:

▶ What you'll need your money for in the future.

▶ When you anticipate needing your money.

▶ How much risk you're willing to accept in order to help your savings grow.

▶ The strength of the economy.

▶ How knowledgeable you are about available investment opportunities and how much time you're willing to dedicate toward managing your investment portfolio.

The biggest difference between investing for long-term expenses (such as buying a home) and your retirement is that all investments that are not retirement-related are typically made using after-tax income. The investment strategies you use (how and where you invest your money), however, may be similar.

If you're planning for retirement, the investment strategies you use should be different than if you're saving for a new home, for example. In terms of retirement planning, there are different tax implications involved with putting funds into a Traditional IRA, Roth IRA, Rollover IRA, Annuity, SEP-IRA, 401(k), Keogh, or other type of retirement account.

Paying for Your Child's Education

The best time to begin saving for your child's education is when they're born, because the cost of attending college is high and continuously increasing. As early as possible, initiate a systematic savings plan. When your child gets close to college-age and starts considering what college he or she will attend, as the parent, you should:

- Figure out how much money you already have available to help pay for the education, based upon your savings, income, and trusts. Determine if additional funds will be needed.

- Immediately explore the availability of scholarships, as well as low-interest student and parent loans. Consider whether or not it makes sense to refinance your home, obtain a second mortgage, or obtain some other type of personal loan.

- Set up a meeting with the College Guidance Counselor at your child's high school and the Financial Aid office at the college or university your child wants to attend.

When considering what funds are available in terms of grants, low-interest loans, and scholarships, fill out the FAFSA (Free Application for Student Aid) forms. You can do this online (*www.fafsa.ed.gov*) or obtain the paperwork at any college's Financial Aid office or any high school's College Guidance Office. The U.S. Department of Education offers a variety of state and federal student financial aid programs. A student's eligibility isn't entirely based on their parents' income.

According to the FAFSA Website: "The Department of Education uses the information provided on your FAFSA to determine your eligibility for aid from the Federal Student Aid programs. Many states and schools also use the FAFSA to award aid from their programs."

Some of the requirements to receive aid from FAFSA programs are that you must:

- Be a citizen or eligible non-citizen of the United States with a valid Social Security number.

- Have a high school diploma, a General Education Development (GED) certificate, or pass an approved "ability to benefit" test.

- Enroll in an eligible program as a regular student seeking a degree or certificate.

- Register (or have registered) for Selective Service, if you are a male between the ages of 18–25.

Between whatever you can afford, student loans, grants, scholarships, and other sources of funding, virtually every person who wants to attend college can, at least from a financial standpoint. To ensure this is possible

106

for your child, start planning early and do plenty of research into government and private funding options. Always focus on the scholarships and grants first, because this is money that won't need to be paid back, and then supplement what your child receives with private funding (savings, loans, and so forth).

One common option is for a child to begin their college career by attending a community college in order to earn credits without incurring a huge expense, and then transfer to a four-year state school or private college or university later. To learn more about all of your options for paying for a college education, contact the Department of Education's Federal Student Aid office (1-800-4-FED-AID or *studentaid.ed.gov*).

Retirement Planning

No matter how old you are, there is no better time to start planning for your retirement than right now. If, through your job, you receive any type of retirement benefits, the way to start your retirement planning is by speaking with the person at your company in charge of handling those benefits. Someone in your company's human resources department will know the right person you should speak with. You might also want to consult with your accountant, Certified Financial Planner, or a retirement specialist (at a company such as Fidelity Investments, Charles Schwab, or your local bank/financial institution).

It's important to begin your retirement planning by developing an understanding of what your needs will be. Next, learn about what benefits you'll be entitled to from Social Security and your employer. You can contact the Social Security Administration at 1-800-722-1213 or *www.ssa.gov* or the U.S. Department of Labor at 1-800-998-7542 or *www.dol.gov*.

The next step is to open some type of tax-sheltered savings plan for your retirement. As part of the benefits package you receive from your employer, you might already have a 401(k) established. A 401(k) plan is a federally approved plan established by your employer that allows you to set aside a percentage of your pay before taxes are taken out. Any growth in the 401(k) is tax-deferred. Once money is in your 401(k), you generally cannot make withdrawals before the age of 59 1/2, except for special circumstances. Many employers, however, include loan provisions in their plans. Many employers offer 401(k) plans in place of a traditional pension.

If your employer doesn't offer a 401(k) or pension plan, you can start contributing to your own retirement fund, such as an IRA (Individual Retirement Account). This is the fastest, most cost-effective, and easiest way to save money for retirement, because the money you contribute now is tax-free (until it's withdrawn), plus you'll earn interest on your investment(s). You can invest $2,000 per year, tax-free into your Traditional IRA. Most banks and financial institutions can help you open an IRA in a matter of minutes. Other retirement plans allow you to invest significantly more of your pre-tax income each year.

Keep in mind, any money you invest into your retirement accounts should not be touched until you reach retirement age. There are stiff financial penalties if you try to get at the money sooner.

The immediate benefits to investing in a retirement plan are that you'll pay lower annual income taxes now, plus you'll be saving money for the future. Be sure to read Appendix A to learn strategies for finding and hiring a financial advisor.

Improve Your Future Income Potential

So far, this book has offered a wide range of strategies for making the most out of the income you're earning currently. However, when looking at the big picture and into the future, you'll want to improve your financial situation by improving your income potential. The next chapter focuses on developing a career plan for yourself that will allow you to maximize your earning potential in the future by earning raises and promotions, better understanding the job market and how you fit into it, and discovering how to pave your career path so you'll be able to improve your standard of living in the months and years to come.

Tomorrow's Reality:
Your Money and You

This book is all about making your paycheck last and helping you better utilize every penny you earn in order to improve your overall quality of life, get out of debt, and help plan for a stable financial future. In this chapter, you'll discover some strategies for improving your income potential *in the future* by carefully planning your career path, starting right now.

While much of what's offered in this book will help you better spend and save the money you have and are currently earning, this chapter will help you make yourself a more valuable asset to your employer, thus assisting you in potentially earning more money. In other words, this chapter offers some long-term career advice and proven strategies that will put you in a much better position to generate more income. As you read this chapter, think about how your professional goals relate to your long-term financial goals, and determine what needs to be achieved in order to make all of your goals a reality. Throughout this chapter, the focus is on setting and achieving long-term professional goals and improving your quality of life in the months and years to come.

Determining Your True Earning Potential

In Chapter 1, you calculated your current net worth and determined your current income. Based on your skills, education, experience, and where you live (your geographic area), are you truly earning what you're worth in today's job market? During tough financial times, employers typically encourage their employees to work harder for little or no extra pay. This is typically an effort to cut costs and boost productivity, and is to be expected. However, is your employer taking advantage of you financially and not paying you what you're actually worth?

Because salaries and compensation packages are typically kept confidential within a company, it can be difficult to determine if you're getting paid what you truly deserve based on your experience, skills, education, geographic area, and what your coworkers are earning.

Whether you're looking for a new job, hoping to earn a raise, or you're convinced you're not getting paid what you're worth at your current job, there are things you can do to discover your true earning potential.

Many things contribute to someone's salary and overall compensation package. Work experience, education, skills, the size of the company, the industry, the geographic location of the employer, demand, the number of hours you work, and your ability to negotiate the best possible salary and compensation package all help to determine what you get paid and what benefits (perks) you receive.

Once you know exactly what type of job you're looking to fill (or you currently fill), you can perform research to determine what salary range someone holding a similar job title with similar responsibilities earns within your industry and geographic area. Using this information, you can then determine if you're currently earning less than what you're worth and take the necessary steps to either pursue a higher-paying job, a raise, or a promotion.

No matter what industry you work in, it's possible to pinpoint average salaries paid by employers for specific jobs. One of the best resources for gathering current and accurate salary information (available online or in printed form) is *The Occupational Outlook Handbook* (*www.bls.gov/oco*), published every two years by The Bureau of Labor Statistics.

The Occupational Outlook Handbook is available at most libraries and the Career Services office at most high schools, colleges and universities, as well as online. For each of the thousands of occupations covered, this directory describes the nature of the work, working conditions, employment opportunities, the job outlook, the earning potential and salary range, as well as information about related occupations.

On the Web, there are many research firms and other sources of salary information. When using these sources for research, however, first determine where the information is derived from, whether or not it's current, and if the data applies to your industry, occupation, and geographic area.

By doing research, it's relatively easy to determine if you're getting paid less than what you're worth in today's market. Knowing exactly what you're worth will help you participate successfully in a salary negotiation with your current or future employer. The following are some excellent online resources for salary information and research:

➤ America's Career InfoNet
   Website: www.acinet.org

   In addition to offering an abundance of news and information about the U.S. job market in general, you can complete a simple questionnaire and receive a personalized salary report, based upon such things as job title, industry, and geographic area.

   America's Career InfoNet also allows users to learn about typical wages and employment trends across occupations and industries; check education, knowledge, skills, and abilities against requirements for most occupations; search for employer contact information nationwide; compare cost of living data; call up state profiles with labor market conditions; plus access nearly 5,500 external links leading to other career resources on the Internet.

➤ Salary.com
   Phone: 1-866-275-2791
   Website: *www.salary.com*

   This comprehensive Website offers a feature called The Salary Wizard. Simply by answering a few questions relating to the job category you're interested in, a job title, and your zip code, you'll receive a free mini-report describing the salary range earned by people with that job title in the geographic area you selected. Salary data relating to thousands of job titles is contained in The Salary Wizard's database, which is updated monthly.

For a one-time fee of $49.95, you can also obtain a highly detailed, 14-page Personal Salary Report. According to the Salary.com Website, (at *http://secure.salary.com/salaryreport/docs/salaryreport/htmls/psr_help. html#premiumdata*), this is:

> "a fully customized document providing our compensation experts' opinion of your market value, based on what you tell Salary.com about your background, experience, and job setting. A Personal Salary Report is designed to help you get the most out of your next salary negotiation—whether it's at a performance review, a job interview, or a promotion."

Through extensive research, Salary.com has determined that someone's salary and compensation is typically based on eight factors. When ordering a Personal Salary Report, you'll be asked for additional information so each of these factors can be taken into consideration. Thus, information you receive will be tailored to you.

Salary.com reports that the eight factors known to have the greatest potential impact on pay are:

› Years of experience.

› Education.

› Last performance rating.

› Person to whom you report.

› Number of people reporting to you.

› Professional organizations and designations.

› Shift.

› Hazardous working conditions.

In addition to the Salary Wizard, Salary.com offers a handful of other free tools, such as a Cost-of-Living Calculator. This tool allows you to compare your earning potential versus the cost of living between where you live now and virtually any other city in America (or another country). Whether you're simply trying to determine what you're worth in today's market or you're actively looking for a new, higher paying job, Salary.com offers timely and valuable information that's easy to access and understand.

➤ JobStar Central

Website: *jobstar.org/tools/salary/sal-prof.cfm*

This is a free service that publishes profession-specific salary surveys online for more than 60 professions, ranging from accounting to warehousing.

➤ The Clayton Wallis Company's CompGeo Service

Phone: 1-707-996-0967

Website: *www.claytonwallis.com/cxgonl.html*

This service offers online information about salaries based on geographic location. For example, if you're working in healthcare, you can determine what people with your qualifications are earning, around the country, using the information offered at this Website. CompGeo offers salary information for more than 1,000 occupations. There is a fee (between $29 and $379) to access some of the more detailed reports this company and Website offers.

➤ Careerjournal.com—Salaries & Profiles

Website: *www.careerjournal.com*

From the publishers of *The Wall Street Journal*, this comprehensive, career-related Website offers a wide range of free services, including its SalaryExpert feature. SalaryExpert allows you to research salary information based upon job titles and geographic areas. The Salary Calculator allows you to compare your earning potential in various cities throughout America.

Improving Your Income Potential

With proper thought and planning, there are a multitude of things you can do over time to improve your earning potential dramatically. As you gain experience on the job, you become a more valuable asset to your employer, and in turn, should be paid more.

Being able to demonstrate an upwardly mobile career path is also important, especially when changing jobs or being considered for a raise or promotion. When an employer (or potential employer) looks at your resume, it should show that with each job or position you've held, you have taken on more responsibilities, learned new skills, gained a wider range of experiences, and earned more money. For example, your career path might involve starting in an entry-level position at your company and then, over a period of years, working your way up to assistant manager, manager, and perhaps vice president of your division. No matter what you do in terms of your career, you should always be working to improve yourself and make yourself more valuable to employers.

In addition to simply staying on the job and working hard, some of the other things you can do to improve your earning potential include:

▶ Improving your personal skill set.

▶ Obtaining additional on-the-job training.

▶ Pursuing a higher level of education.

▶ Becoming a more responsible employee.

▶ Making a greater effort to assist others (coworkers and superiors) while on the job and actively demonstrating your value to superiors.

▶ Improving your attitude.

Improving Your Personal Skill Set

When applying for virtually any type of job, at some point in the process you'll be provided with a description of the position. This will be a listing of the core skills and requirements needed by you, the applicant, according to what the employer perceives its expectations and needs to be. Often, specific education, work experience, or skills will be listed for the position.

As the job seeker or employee, it's important to position and market your personal skill set so it's in line with exactly what the employer is looking for. While simply meeting the job's requirements in terms of your skill set is a requirement, to enhance your marketability as an applicant and perhaps enhance your earning potential, you'll want to carefully market yourself to a potential employer by showcasing *all* of your related skills.

What is your personal skill set? Your personal and professional skill set can be any knowledge or ability that makes you a more desirable and productive person on the job. Depending on the industry you work in or the type of position you're looking to fill, your skill set goes beyond the core education you received in school. It includes the skills that ultimately allow you to meet the responsibilities of your specific job.

In today's job market, computer literacy, for example, is an important skill. To truly market this skill, you'll want to promote your knowledge of specific programs and operating systems. For example, proficiency using Microsoft Office XP and all of its programs (Word, Excel, PowerPoint, Explorer, and so on) is an extremely desirable and marketable skill for someone looking to work in a traditional office or corporate environment. Likewise, knowing how to utilize the Internet and e-mail are important skills many employers look for.

While the skills desired by employers will vary greatly, based on your occupation, some examples of marketable skills include:

▶ Analytical thinking.

▶ Being a creative thinker.

▶ Being a good listener.

▶ Being a team player.

▶ Being deadline-oriented.

▶ Being task-oriented.

▶ Computer literacy.

▶ Effective prioritization and time management.

▶ Excellent written communication.

▶ Knowledge of Microsoft Office programs (or other popular computer software).

▶ Leadership.

▶ Mathematical competancy.

▶ Organization.

▶ Polished telephone communication.

▶ Public speaking.

▶ Seasoned sales abilities.

▶ Self-motivation.

▸ Strong interpersonal communication.

▸ Strong work ethic.

▸ Telemarketing experience.

▸ The ability to adapt quickly to changing priorities.

▸ The ability to effectively close sales within a business (or retail) environment.

▸ The ability to execute and plan strategies.

▸ The ability to multitask.

▸ The ability to use specific types of equipment directly related to your job/industry.

▸ The ability to work with all levels of management.

▸ Thorough research abilities.

Once you know what type of job you're applying for and have a general idea of what the employer is looking for, your cover letter, resume, and employment application all provide excellent opportunities to quickly show-case your personal and professional skill set.

The "help wanted" ad or job description provided by the potential employer will offer valuable clues regarding the specific skills you should possess and which ones are of particular importance to an employer. Determine exactly what the employer is looking for before you devise a plan on how to best promote your skill set.

Simply stating you have a skill that's required for a job isn't enough. You'll need to clearly spell out every skill you have that's directly relevant to the job you're applying for, then be able to provide specific examples of how you've already used each skill in a previous work situation. In other words, proof that you posses each skill is essential. As you list each skill and describe how you've used it on the job, provide specific quantitative and qualitative details that convey the positive results of your abilities.

Every marketable skill you posses has a value to an employer. Thus, having more skills than what's specifically spelled out by the employer will make you more desirable. It's your responsibility to demonstrate exactly how your particular combination of skills will make you a valuable asset to an employer. While focusing on those skills that are directly relevant to the position you're applying for, try to expand the focus of your abilities so it becomes obvious to an employer that you have the skills already in place to take on additional responsibilities in the future.

Developing and improving upon your skill set should be an ongoing endeavor. Some of the best ways to learn new skills is by:

- ▶ Attending adult education classes at night or on weekends.

- ▶ Joining specific organizations. For example, if you're interested in improving your public speaking skills, Toastmasters International (*www.toastmasters.org* or 1-949-858-8255) is an excellent organization to become involved with.

- ▶ Listening to audio courses or watching video courses. If you're looking to improve your vocabulary, for instance, an audio program called Verbal Advantage (*www.verbaladvantage.com* or 1-800-765-5522) can help you build your vocabulary. Word Success, LLC, the company that developed Verbal Advantage, also offers audio courses that teach business writing, conversational skills, and listening skills. Nightingale-Conant (*www.nightingale.com* or 1-800-525-9000) is another well-known company that publishes hundreds of audio and video programs designed to help people develop their personal and professional skill set. Audiocassette (or audio CD) programs can even be listened to in the car during your commute to and from work or while working out at the gym, using a Walkman.

- ▶ Participating in on-the-job training.

- ▶ Participating in seminars at trade shows.

- ▶ Reading self-help and how-to books.

Once you learn the core skill(s) you want and need, keep practicing them in your personal and professional life. No amount of reading or classroom instruction, for example, can replace hands-on experience using a particular skill. The more you use a skill, the more proficient at it you'll become.

Obtain Additional On-the-Job Training

Many employers offer on-the-job training. If you have the option to receive paid or unpaid training in order to learn skills needed for your own job or for positions you plan to hold in the future, take full advantage of whatever training is offered. In many cases, employers will pay for your training, plus compensate you for the time you spend being trained. Any education you obtain, new skills you learn, or new experiences you acquire, will all contribute to making you a more valuable employee and increase your earning potential.

Pursuing a Higher Level of Education

An education is something that nobody can ever take away from you. Virtually all employers put a premium value on education. Depending on the type of career you're pursuing, at the very least you'll be required to have a high school diploma or GED. However, if you have a two-year college degree, a four-year college degree, a graduate school education, a professional license, and/or a professional accreditation, your earning potential almost automatically increases dramatically.

Just because you're working full-time, don't think that pursuing a college or advanced degree (or professional license or accreditation) is beyond the scope of possibility. If you're willing to attend classes at night or on weekends, you can obtain the education you want or need. Even if your finances are extremely limited, you can attend a community college, which is less expensive, plus receive financial aid, grants, scholarships, and/or student loans. Contrary to popular belief, financial aid for education is not automatically linked to your income or previous academic performance.

Once you obtain a college degree, you're immediately qualified for higher paying jobs in whatever industry you currently work. Even if completing college will take you two, four, six, or more years (attending part-time), by planning for the future and making the necessary commitment now, you can help guarantee your future financial well-being.

For additional information about obtaining federal- and state-issued student loans or financial aid, contact the financial aid office at any school, college, or university. You can also visit the FAFSA (Free Application for Federal Student Aid) Website at *www.fafsa.ed.gov*.

Becoming a More Responsible Employee

Are you someone who watches the clock at work? Do you show up exactly when you're supposed to and leave the moment your workday is scheduled to end? Do you take on only those work-related responsibilities you're required to and nothing more? In today's competitive business world, your attitude and performance are as important as the knowledge, skills, and experience you possess. Simply by demonstrating your dedication to your job and, when necessary, doing above and beyond what's expected of you, you will be perceived as a more valuable employee.

Without being taken advantage of by your employer, make a point to take on additional responsibilities, learn the responsibilities of your co-workers and superiors, and show that you're willing to work hard on an ongoing basis. Your attitude will become apparent to your employer. Over time, you will be relied upon more, perhaps becoming indispensable to your superiors. Thus, when you're evaluated periodically for bonuses, raises, and promotions, you'll be more apt to receive what you deserve, allowing you to improve your income potential.

Your Attitude Counts Too!

In addition to becoming more responsible, focus on your attitude. How do your coworkers and superiors perceive you? When an employer evaluates an employee for a possible raise or promotion, his or her overall attitude will always be considered. Make an effort to demonstrate an upbeat, motivated, responsible, professional, and friendly attitude while on the job.

Demonstrate Your Value to Superiors

As you work hard at whatever job you possess, keep an ongoing journal that documents your accomplishments and the work you do that's above and beyond what's required of you. Don't simply assume that your superiors know everything you do for them and for your company. Your superior may be managing dozens, perhaps hundreds of other employees. It is your responsibility to ensure that you document your accomplishments, especially in conjunction with employee evaluations or when you're pursuing a raise or promotion. Make sure you're receiving the credit for the work you do and that nobody is taking credit for your hard work.

Earning a Raise or Promotion

These days, people typically change employers multiple times throughout their career. Gone are the days when you'd graduate from school, land a job with a major corporation, and stay with that company until you retire with a gold watch. Whether you're changing employers or simply looking to earn a raise or promotion with your current employer, it's important to constantly move your career path forward and pursue upward mobility. Thus, when you land a new job, one of your first questions should relate to what it will take to earn a raise or promotion. Once you know what needs to be done, start working hard to achieve those requirements. This is one of the best ways to ensure your income will increase over time. Don't simply rely on the cost of living increases or bonuses your employer may or may not offer if you stay in your current position for years at a time. Instead, work toward earning a higher paying job.

Raises and promotions are typically not awarded based upon whether or not your boss likes you. While personalities do come into play, a company's focus will always be on its bottom line. What the employer will be asking is, "Are you worth what we're paying you or plan to pay you?" As long as your value to the employer is equal to or greater than what you're being paid, your chances of earning the raise or promotion you want will be easier to achieve. Remember, you'll often need to actively demonstrate your value on an ongoing basis to your employer. Simply showing up for work on time during the week you're scheduled for your periodic employee review isn't enough to earn you the promotion and pay raise you want.

If you've been with a company for more than one year, have become a valuable employee, yet aren't being paid what you truly believe you're worth, it might become necessary to take matters into your own hands and ask for (not demand) a raise. When it comes to asking for a raise, you always want to take a highly professional approach and should never become overly emotional or confrontational with your employer. One of the biggest mistakes people make when asking for a raise is that they deliver an ultimatum, stating something such as "Give me a raise, or I'll quit." Unless you're absolutely willing to quit on the spot, this should not be the tactic you use.

Before approaching your superior about getting a raise, review your work history and write down all of your professional accomplishments while working for your current employer. Include on your list specific examples of how you've become a valuable asset to the company and to your superiors. How much new business have you brought to the company? How much have you helped to increase productivity? What impact have you had on the company's overall success? How much unpaid overtime have you put in during the past six months? You won't be showing the employer this list, but it'll help dramatically in your preparation.

120

Virtually all employers evaluate employees based on their overall track record when it comes to hard work, ongoing dedication, and long-term productivity. The bottom-line issue the employer will be concerned with is whether you are worth the salary you want to be paid. Is it worth it for the company to make an added investment in you, or is it better off, from a financial standpoint, to invest in another employee? Being able to provide credible arguments in your favor when you meet with the employer will help you land the raise you're looking for.

Asking for a raise can be very stressful. The best way to eliminate this stress is to be totally prepared. If you don't honestly believe that you deserve a raise, you'll have a very hard time convincing your employer. Remember, you have nothing to lose if your request is denied, so go into your meeting with confidence.

After you have developed your list of reasons why you deserve a raise, make a formal appointment with your boss. Don't just walk into his or her office and make your request. Schedule the meeting during a time when you know your boss will be the least stressed and the most open-minded. Your chances for getting a raise will be better if the company is currently doing well and if you were somehow recently involved in a major project, sales effort, or assignment that was successful.

As your meeting begins, outline your accomplishments and contributions to the company. Focus on how much you enjoy working for the company, and how much you believe you'll be able to contribute in the future. Never complain about your personal problems or bring up your personal debts as the reason you need a raise. Your best strategy is to focus on how much and why you deserve a raise—not how much you want or need a raise.

Never assume your employer has full knowledge of your accomplishments and contributions to the company. After reviewing this information during your meeting, it's time to ask for a salary increase. Before stating how much of a raise you're looking for, you should do research to determine how much other people in comparable jobs are earning at your company and at other companies in your industry.

Always avoid arguments or getting yourself into a defensive position. Focus only on your strengths, without making excuses for weaknesses that your employer may bring up as reasons why you don't deserve a raise.

During your meeting, be prepared to negotiate. An employer may consider a proposed 10-percent salary increase out of the question, but might be open to an immediate 5-percent raise, with an additional guaranteed 5-percent raise within a year. If your request is denied, ask questions to determine what, specifically, it would take for you to earn a raise and when the employer would consider evaluating you again to make the determination. Knowing specifics will help you achieve what the employer is looking for.

Whether or not you receive a raise is almost always a financial issue for the employer, not a personal one, so if you don't receive a raise, don't get angry or overly emotional in front of the employer. Aside from receiving additional financial compensation, you might still be able to negotiate better benefits or incentives. For example, if the employer agrees that you deserve a raise, but states that it's not currently in the budget, ask for extra vacation days or a higher commission rate (if you're in a sales-oriented job). Benefits are worth money, so while negotiating a better benefits package won't put cash in your wallet, it will improve the overall quality of your life.

If your request for a raise is flatly denied, yet you're convinced you're worth more as an employee, consider looking for a new job, but don't quit your existing job until you've lined up a new one. After receiving new job offers, it may be appropriate to offer your current employer one last opportunity to increase your salary before quitting, but that's a personal decision on your part. Sometimes choosing to pursue a new career opportunity will offer greater financial benefits, but try to maintain a positive professional relationship with the employer you're leaving.

Paving Your Career Path

Based on what you do for a living, conduct some research to determine what career path options are available and then pave your own career path accordingly. Create a one-, three-, five-, 10-, and 15-year plan for yourself, based on what people in your industry are typically able to achieve.

By evaluating the accomplishments of your superiors and executives within your company, you should be able to determine what skills, education, experiences, and job titles they've held in the past as they climbed the corporate ladder to their current position. If your goal is to follow in the footsteps of your company's current executive vice president, and you're in an entry-level position with the company, you need to create a career path for yourself that will keep you motivated and moving toward your goal.

If you determine that your company's current executive vice president has been with the company for 10 years and has held specific job titles, try to duplicate their successes and follow in their footsteps.

Likewise, if you're earning $28,000 per year now, but in 10 years you want to be earning $45,000 per year, determine what additional skills, education, and experiences you'll need to be qualified for a position at your desired salary level. Knowing that you have 10 years to achieve your objective, develop a plan in which you'll systematically move up the corporate ladder, one rung at a time, over the next decade.

Finding Employment in a Tough Economy

When the economy is bad, companies tend to downsize, leaving thousands, perhaps millions of hard-working people without jobs. If you sense your job isn't as secure as it once was, don't wait until you're fired to start looking for new employment opportunities. It's always easier to find a job while you're still employed, because you're not under pressure and you have time to find the best possible opportunities. It is certainly possible to conduct a job search without your current employer being aware of your efforts. However, if you do this, never use the telephone or Internet connection you have at work to conduct your job search efforts.

If you're suddenly forced to find work in a tough economy, it's vital that you pursue every possible option to find new job opportunities. Simply responding to "help wanted" ads or posting your resume on a career-related Website isn't enough.

"Help wanted" ads, the Internet, attending job fairs, and visiting the Career Counseling office at your college or university are all excellent resources for finding job opportunities. One of the most powerful job search tools at your disposal, however, is your ability to network.

Networking can take on many forms. While many consider it a skill, networking can be easily mastered, allowing virtually anyone with friends, family, former coworkers, and professional acquaintances to find the best job opportunities, simply by striking up conversations with people and asking for assistance and/or referrals.

Because upwards of 80 percent of all job openings are never advertised, networking is one of the best ways to explore what many call the "hidden job market." As you begin your job search, contact people you know, starting with people currently working in the industry you hope to work in.

123

From the people you network with, you can typically:

▸ Discover unadvertised job openings.

▸ Get referrals for other people to speak with about possible job openings.

▸ Get your foot in the door at a company by having someone make a personal introduction.

▸ Learn about specific companies (potential employers).

▸ Meet others working in the industry that interests you.

▸ Obtain a letter of recommendation.

▸ Receive career advice and guidance.

Clients, customers, and other people you know from current or past jobs can also be incorporated into your networking circle and tapped when it comes to finding job opportunities.

If you're first starting to develop a network, some of the other people you should consider contacting are people with occupations requiring them to deal or associate with many other customers or clients, from all walks of life. For example, build your networking circle by speaking with:

▸ Accountants (with clients in a wide range of industries).

▸ Bankers.

▸ Church friends/clergy.

▸ College friends.

▸ Commuting acquaintances.

▸ Doctors.

▸ Doormen/security guards at office buildings.

▸ Employees of companies you'd be interested in working for.

▸ Fitness club acquaintances.

▸ Hairstylists and barbers.

▸ Lawyers.

▸ Past teachers/deans.

▸ Your high school or college alumni association.

▸ Your local Chamber of Commerce.

If you don't know anyone working in your particular industry, write down the names of between 10 and 25 friends, relatives, and acquaintances you could call right now in order to ask about job leads or assistance in finding a new job. Even if you call each person on your list and none of them is able to help you directly, you're virtually guaranteed that someone on your list will know someone else who can help you find and land the job you're looking for.

When you correspond with a network contact that isn't a close friend or relative, be sure to refresh that person's memory about how they know you, and when/where you met. If a friend tells you that one of their other friends can probably help you, make a point to first meet that person before asking for his or her assistance.

Be sure to briefly explain to your network contact(s) exactly what type of job you're looking for, and provide him or her with a short summary of your most impressive work experience and skills. You want your contacts to know something about you, so they can speak highly of you to their superiors, coworkers, or people in their network of friends and associates. Developing a network is an ongoing process. Even after landing a job, you'll find these people will prove beneficial throughout your career.

Utilizing your networking skills to tap the hidden job market is an excellent way of finding higher-paying job opportunities that you're qualified to fill.

When to Consider Changing Careers or Relocating

Not everyone makes the right career-related decisions when they graduate from school and enter the workforce for the first time. It's common for people to find themselves in jobs they hate or that don't allow them to earn the income they desire.

After a few years in the workplace, perhaps you realize you should have pursued a totally different career path, in a different industry. In this situation, while you're still employed, conduct research to determine what additional skills, education, and experience you'd require to land a job in a field you'd be more interested in. Next, develop a plan that will allow you to meet those job requirements. There are two major reasons why people

125

choose to change careers (not simply change jobs). First, they realize they could earn significantly more money doing something else. Second, they hate what they're doing now, and choose to pursue something they're interested in and that they'd enjoy. Ideally, if you're changing careers, it should be for both of these reasons.

Another common problem people face is that they ultimately find themselves working in a dead-end job with little or no upward mobility. Because a job with no future growth potential means no predictable increase in income in the future, it might be a good idea to consider a job change.

Often, whether you're changing jobs or changing careers, you'll be able to find the job opportunity you're looking for near where you currently live—but not always. To find the perfect job opportunity, you may need to extend your search to neighboring towns or cities, or perhaps other states. Before accepting a job that will require you to relocate, consider how the move will impact your personal life (and the life of your spouse and children).

Next, consider the cost of living where you may be moving to and how your new salary would compare to your current salary, based on the difference in the cost of living where you'll potentially be moving.

Suppose you live and work in New York City and earn $45,000 per year, but you're offered a similar job in Cedar Rapids, Iowa. According to Salary.com's Cost-of-Living Wizard, in February 2003:

> "The cost of living in Cedar Rapids, Iowa, is 49.4 percent lower than in New York City. Therefore, you would have to earn a salary of only $22,781 [not $45,000] to maintain your current standard of living. Employers in Cedar Rapids, Iowa, typically pay 15.1 percent less than employers in New York City. Therefore, if you take the same type of job working for the same type of company, you are likely to earn $38,220 [not $45,000]."

You would, however, still have a $15,439 net change in disposable income (money left over after all of your living expenses are covered), so if you're willing to move to Iowa, this could be a financially worthwhile decision.

There are situations, however, in which the cost of living will increase dramatically in the city you plan to move to. Thus, even though you may be receiving a small pay increase, your quality of life would decrease or stay the same, because living in that city will be more expensive. To avoid this, do research in advance. Use a cost-of-living calculator to help you determine the difference between how much it costs to live where you are now versus where you plan to move.

Try to make your decision about a career change or a relocation based upon the personal benefits as well as the financial ones. Moving 1,500 miles away from your friends and close relatives simply for a higher paying job may not be worth it to you. Likewise, disrupting the lives of your children by forcing them to change schools and leave their friends may not be worth the additional money you could earn by moving. Prior to making the decision about moving, consider all of the personal, professional, and financial ramifications, and then act accordingly so what you do is in your best interest.

Other Sources of Incomes

If times get particularly tough, it may make financial sense for you to keep your current job but also pursue other sources of income, perhaps by taking on a second, part-time job, making your investments work harder to generate better returns, or by starting your own home-based or Internet-based business during your free time.

Particularly during the holiday season, many people take on a second job in retail, because so many retail stores (including major department stores) hire extra seasonal employees and offer excellent bonuses and benefits, plus highly flexible work hours.

Some people choose to supplement their primary income by starting a home-based, consulting, or Internet-based business or consulting practice. If done correctly, these ventures can be lucrative. However, the time commitment required is often substantial and you may need to make an initial financial investment to get your business started. Prior to starting your own business, do research and obtain the knowledge and skills you'll need to manage the day-to-day operations of your business. Also, have in-depth conversations with other entrepreneurs so you develop a good understanding of the commitment involved.

If you have a good idea for a business as well as the knowledge, skills, and resources to make the business viable, this is an option for increasing your income that should not be ignored. There are countless stories of home-based business operators, for example, transforming their small, part-time businesses into successful, full-time careers over time. Likewise, people have discovered ways of generating significant incomes by tapping the power of the Internet. For some, buying and selling items on eBay or other online auctions sites can be a viable part-time way of generating additional income.

Putting the Pieces All Together

Whatever your current financial situation, hopefully this book has helped you take control of your current income by teaching you simple ways to make your paycheck last. To improve your overall financial situation, however, you'll ultimately need to control or eliminate your debt, develop and implement a budget for yourself, carefully plan your investments, begin saving, and plan for the future (including for your retirement). None of these activities takes too much time, yet by taking the necessary steps right now, you'll be able to improve your financial situation dramatically.

This book provided the basic information you need to get started on your own path toward long-term financial security. What's required now is your dedication to putting the information you've learned into practice. Once you develop your budget, you need to force yourself to stick to it in order to achieve the desired results. Finally, as you embark on your path toward financial security, don't be afraid to seek out the help of finance experts. These people have the professional knowledge you may lack.

Hopefully you have discovered that anyone, even you, can quickly take control over your finances and implement a handful of ways to make your paycheck last. As you experiment with the techniques and strategies described in this book, don't try everything at once. Pick one or two strategies at a time and successfully implement them, then move on to other strategies. Your chances of achieving the financial status you desire will be much easier if you take a well-organized and step-by-step approach. Now that you know what has to be done, go back and prioritize what needs to be done first and take the appropriate actions, starting today!

Appendix B will help you develop specific action plans and take steps toward achieving your financial goals in the short and long term. Remember, no matter how much money you ultimately earn and how you decide to utilize those funds, money does not define who you are as a person!

Appendix A

Get the Financial Help and Advice You Need

While learning how to better manage your money, cutting expenses, and making your paycheck last is now something you can probably do on your own after reading this book, your overall financial well-being is important. So if you still have questions or need advice, seek out the financial help you need! In other words, if you have a question, don't guess at the answer. Make all of your financial decisions based upon the knowledge you acquire and actual facts—not assumptions, guesses, and incorrect financial calculations.

In this section, you'll find 10 tips for hiring a financial specialist, plus discover some of the places to turn for additional financial advice and guidance, especially for things such as dealing with financial emergencies, taxes, managing your investment portfolio, and planning for your retirement.

Depending on your specific questions or concerns, the type of "expert" or "specialist" you should contact will vary. Here's a brief summary of the types of financial professionals who can provide information and guidance, for a fee, of course:

➤ **Accountant/CPA (Certified Public Accountant)/PFS (Personal Financial Specialist)**—Some public accountants, most CPAs, and all CPAs with a PFS certification, can assist you with *all* aspects of your financial needs, including overseeing your investment strategies, planning for your retirement, preparing and filing your tax returns, and planning and implementing a personal or family budget. An accountant, CPA, or PFS will typically charge by the hour for their services. Someone with a CPA or PFS accreditation has obtained extensive training in multiple areas of finance. Overseen by the American Institute of Certified Public Accountants (AICPA), in order for someone to earn a CPA accreditation, he or she must complete a program of study in accounting at an accredited college or university. Part of this education includes at least 150 semester hours of college study necessary to obtain the general knowledge needed to become a CPA. Upon completion of the coursework and a predetermined amount of professional work experience in public accounting, it is necessary to pass the Uniform CPA Examination—a licensing exam developed by the AICPA that is also graded by the organization.

A CPA specializes in tax-related issues at the income, estate, and trust levels. They are usually qualified to deal with some or all of the tax and financial planning aspects of developing an estate or trust plan (but not draw up the actual documents, which can only be done by a practicing lawyer). A CPA specializing in taxes is usually qualified to deal with federal, state, and local tax agencies if you have fallen behind in your business or personal income tax payments and need someone to assist you or represent you in negotiations with those tax agencies. For more information or a referral, contact the AICPA (1-888-777-7077 or *www.aicpa.org/index.htm*) or your state's CPA society.

➤ **Certified Financial Planner (CFP)**—According to the Certified Financial Planner Board of Standards Website (*http://www.cfp.net/Upload/Publications/181.pdf*):

> "Financial planning is the process of determining how an individual can meet life goals through the proper management of his or her financial resources. A financial planner is someone who uses the financial planning process to help clients figure out how to meet their life goals. A financial planner can take a 'big-picture' view of a client's financial situation and make financial planning recommendations based on the client's needs in areas such as budgeting and saving, taxes, investments, insurance, and retirement planning. Or, the planner may work with a client on a single financial

issue, but within the context of that client's overall situation. A financial planner helps a client analyze either all or selected areas of his or her finances and develops a plan, thus bringing together all of the client's financial goals. This big-picture approach to a client's financial goals sets the planner apart from other financial advisers, who may have been trained to focus on a particular area of a client's financial life."

A CFP usually has less formal related education and training than a CPA. A CFP, however, typically costs less to hire. Often, a CFP may be less independent, because he or she may be tied to financial product related companies (such as insurance, brokerage firms, or mutual fund companies). For more information or a referral, contact the Certified Financial Planner Board of Standards (1-888-237-6275 or *www.cfp-board.org*).

➤ **Credit Counseling/Debt Management (Consolidation)**—There are many nonprofit services designed to help you solve serious credit problems by helping you consolidate your debt and negotiate with creditors such as credit card issuers. You've probably seen ads for companies that offer credit counseling or debt management on TV or in newspapers. Some firms offer services for free, while others charge a (sometimes significant) fee. If you choose to work with this type of organization, make sure you find one that's reputable and can help you with your particular financial problem. There are many debt-reduction scams out there that people fall prey to. Prior to hiring or working with this type of firm, contact the Better Business Bureau in your area to ensure its legitimacy. In some cases, these companies will simply try to convince you to transfer your credit card balances into a single consolidation loan which it provides (and earns interest and fees from). For more information or a referral, contact The Consumer Credit Counseling Service (1-800-388-2227 or *www.cccsatl.org*), visit the DebtAdvice.org Website (*www.debtadvice.org*), or contact The National Foundation for Credit Counseling, Inc. (1-800-388-2227 or *www.nfcc.org*).

➤ **Stockbroker/Investment Planner/Personal Investment Portfolio Manager**—These are people who buy and sell stocks, bonds, mutual funds, and other investments on behalf of their clients. Typically, these people earn a commission based on the investments they buy and sell

131

for each client, and/or earn a fee for managing a client's portfolio. If selected carefully, these professionals can usually help you develop and manage a portfolio based on your long-term financial goals, such as buying a home, paying for a child's college education, and planning for retirement. For more information or a referral, contact the National Association of Securities Dealers (1-800-289-9999 or *www.nasdr.com*).

➤ **Tax Attorney**—If you fall behind in paying your federal, state, and local income taxes, you may need to hire a tax attorney (or a CPA with a tax specialty) to help you deal directly with the IRS. A tax attorney is a lawyer with extensive knowledge of tax issues. Often, they or their legal associates can also help you deal with the financial and legal issues relating to the creation or amendment of your will, creating trusts, and estate planning. For more information or a referral, contact the Bar Association in your state.

Once you know the type of help you need, it's always best to seek out a referral from someone you know and trust. You could also find listings for qualified financial professionals in the Yellow Pages, by searching the Internet, or by seeking a referral from a professional association. Most of these professionals will offer a free initial consultation to help you determine if their services are appropriate to your needs.

Many well-known and reputable financial organizations, such as H&R Block (1-800-HR-BLOCK or *www.hrblock.com*), Fidelity Investments (1-800-343-3548 or *www.fidelity.com*), and Charles Schwab (1-877-488-6762 or *www.schwab.com*), for example, now offer a wide range of relatively inexpensive financial services, plus the convenience of having specialists available in offices nationwide, via the telephone or online. There are also countless independent financial professionals working in your geographic area.

10 Tips for Hiring a Financial Specialist

McGladrey & Pullen, LLP is one of the 10 largest independent CPA firms in the United States. In conjunction with its affiliate, RSM McGladrey, Inc. (1-212-986-3900 or *www.mcgladrey.com*) it's the fifth largest accounting and consulting firm in the United States. During the past 75 years, the firm has grown from two offices in eastern Iowa to having more than 4,000 employees working from more than 100 offices across the country.

Victor S. Rich, CPA, is a Senior Partner of McGladrey & Pullen, LLP and a Senior Managing Director of RSM McGladrey Inc.'s New York offices. In this section, he shares his more than 35 years experience working as a CPA and offers the following 10 tips for hiring any type of financial specialist.

1. Determine your specific needs. Do you need help managing your everyday budget, getting yourself out of debt, planning for your retirement, dealing with tax issues, assisting you in your divorce action, preparing your tax returns, creating an investment strategy, or help with estate planning? Each one of these issues requires a different expertise. Make sure you're hiring the right person for the job.

2. Determine the financial specialist's credentials. The generic term "financial planner" can apply to any number of services. A Certified Public Accountant or Certified Financial Planner, for example, requires extensive education and training to achieve this credential. Others who use the "financial planner" title may possess little or no specialized training, nor any credentials or accreditations. Make sure the person has earned the credentials and/or accreditations he or she needs and claims to have. Also, if you're hiring a CPA, confirm that he or she is a member in good standing of a professional organization, such as the American Institute of Certified Public Accountants, or a relevant state CPA society.

3. Determine what services are actually offered by the person you're looking to hire. Does he or she have the necessary experience to handle your particular issues or concerns? Seek out a referral from someone you know and then ask for at least three recent referrals. Don't be timid about asking for references and then following up. You don't want the wrong person giving you the wrong advice.

4. Determine specifically what type of approach the specialist will be taking. Do you agree with their approach for dealing with your financial situation? If, for example, you're hiring someone to manage your investment portfolio, are you comfortable with the level of risk the specialist will be taking with your money? Are you comfortable that you will not be too large or too small of a client for the consultant you are about to select?

5. If you're hiring a firm, determine who, specifically, you will be working with. Will you have direct access to this person? Make sure you're comfortable with the person you'll be working with and you believe you can trust that person. After all, you will be disclosing the most intimate details of your personal and family finances (as well as other matters) to this person.

6. Understand exactly how and when the financial consultant will be compensated. Will you be paying a flat hourly fee, an hourly fee plus expenses, contingency fees, commissions, or a combination of the aforementioned? For an investment advisor or stockbroker, for example, your fee may be a percentage of your portfolio's total value, a percentage of your portfolio's increase in value, commissions based on the purchase or sale of assets, or some combination. Make sure you understand the fee structure for the person you hire and obtain a written estimate in advance (after an initial consultation). If you are hiring an independent consultant, make sure his or her compensation is fee-based, according to a fixed hourly rate paid only by you for your engagement.

7. Provide the appropriate information to the specialist. Make sure the information you provide to the financial specialist is complete, accurate, and provided in a timely manner. Determine what information and financial records you will have to provide in order for this individual to do his or her job properly.

8. Understand the timeline for working with the financial specialist. What is the turn-around time for services you need to have performed? Is there a specific date or dates by which certain work must be completed? Also, try to determine how promptly the person you hire will return phone calls or respond to your e-mails.

9. Make sure you can develop an ongoing dialog with the person you hire and that you communicate well with each other. When you're given any type of financial advice, it's important to understand what's being said. Does the person explain everything to you properly, in a manner and at a level you understand?

10. Determine what the short-term and long-term benefits to you will be of hiring a specific financial specialist or tax preparation service. Will you save money on taxes by hiring an accountant or having an accounting firm such as H&R Block prepare and file your tax returns? Will you earn a significantly higher rate of return on your investments by hiring someone to manage your portfolio? Does the person have knowledge and experience that you don't? Will this knowledge and expertise allow you to solve a particular financial problem, deal more effectively with a financial crisis, or create a better financial plan? Finally, will hiring that person improve your overall financial situation and will the anticipated benefits to be derived outweigh the cost(s) involved? If the answer is yes, then hire that person now.

Appendix B

Your Monthly Action Plan

As you begin putting your finances in order and taking steps to get the most out of your paycheck, each month you'll want to ensure that you're following one or more predefined game plans. These plans should help you work toward accomplishing your short-term and long-term financial goals.

Each month, answer the following questions and keep detailed records of your progress as well as any new financial challenges and obstacles you encounter. Be sure to modify your action plans as needed in order to stay focused on achieving your objectives. Start developing your monthly plans by answering these questions:

How do you plan to reduce your larger, long-term expenses (mortgage/rent, car payment, insurance premiums, and so on)?

Individual Step to Be Taken	Deadline for Taking This Step	Anticipated Savings ($)	Actual Result(s)/ Savings for the Month

What specific steps will you take to cut everyday expenses?

Individual Step to Be Taken	Deadline for Taking This Step	Anticipated Savings ($)	Actual Result(s)/ Savings for the Month

What steps will you take to reduce and, ultimately, eliminate your debt?

Individual Step to Be Taken	Deadline for Taking This Step	Anticipated Savings ($)	Actual Result(s)/ Savings for the Month

What steps will you take to establish and maintain your emergency fund (savings) and prepare for unexpected financial events?

Individual Step to Be Taken	Deadline for Taking This Step	Anticipated Savings ($)	Actual Result(s)/ Savings for the Month

What steps will you take this month to prepare for your
financial future—your long-term financial planning (retirement,
saving for a new home, saving for a car, paying for your child's
education, and so forth)?

Individual Step to Be Taken	Deadline for Taking This Step	Anticipated Savings ($)	Actual Result(s)/ Savings for the Month

How will you utilize (spend or invest) your disposable income for the month?

Individual Step to Be Taken	Deadline for Taking This Step	Amt. of Change in Disposable Income for the Month	Anticipated Result(s)	Actual Result(s) for the Month

What will you do this month to help you increase your earning
potential in the months and years to come?

Individual Step to Be Taken	Deadline for Taking This Step	Anticipated Outcome	Actual Result(s) for the Month

Will you be hiring any type of financial specialist?

Specitic Problem You're Seeking Help For	Type of Financial Specialist You Will Hire	Timeline or Deadline	Expected Results	Actual Result(s)	Fee(s) Paid for the Service

Index

About the Author

Jason R. Rich (*www.JasonRich.com*) is the best-selling author of more than 25 books on a wide range of topics. His recently published books include *Will You Marry Me? Popping the Question With Romance and Style* (New Page Books), *Brain Storm: Tap Into Your Creativity to Generate Awesome Ideas and Remarkable Results* (The Career Press), and a series of travel guides targeted to families.

When working on any book project, Jason's philosophy is to conduct a tremendous amount of research on the topic at hand, then conduct interviews with the best known and most knowledgeable experts in the world, in order to provide his readers with timely, accurate, and easy-to-understand information that's relevant and immediately useful.

Now in his mid-30s, Jason Rich has been working as a journalist and in the business world for more than 17 years. He's an accomplished author; newspaper and magazine columnist; and provides marketing, PR, and consulting services to numerous businesses in a wide range of industries. He lives just outside of Boston and can be reached via e-mail at jr7777@aol.com.

More useful reference books to improve your skills and knowledge from Career Press.

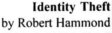

Printed in the United States
79284LV00006B/90

9 781564 146991